They Were My Friends - JACK, BOB AND TED
My life in and out of Politics

Gerard F. Doherty

Omni Publishing Co.
2017

They Were My Friends - JACK, BOB AND TED
My life in and out of Politics

Gerard F. Doherty

Omni Publishing Co.
2017

Published by
Omni Publishing Co.
www.omni-pub.com

Library of Congress cataloging-in-publication data
Doherty, Gerard F.
They Were My Friends – Jack, Bob and Ted
My Life In and Out of Politics
ISBN: 978-0-692-93291-9

Printed in the United States of America
Signature Book Printing, www.sbpbooks.com

Design by: Leonard Massiglia

To My Wife Marilyn

Table of Contents

Chapter 4

Chapter 5

Chapter 6

Foreword

At its best, American politics is personal, deeply rooted in living rooms, town halls, main streets and community centers across the country. It is a pastime carried through generations by neighbors and friends all working to leave their world a little better and kinder than they found it.

In Massachusetts, this fiercely local approach to politics is in our blood. Few people better embody that than my friend, Gerard Doherty. From his very first campaign for the State House in 1954 to my great-uncle, Senator Ted Kennedy's, campaign for president, Gerry has always understood a few golden rules of public service: Don't forget where you came from. Don't forget why you started. And don't forget the names and faces that helped you along the way.

Whether on the streets of his beloved Charlestown or in the neighborhoods of Gary, Indiana, Gerry has been by my family's side through triumph and tragedy. Time and again he offers a sturdy shoulder when you stumble, a bit of wisdom when you're lost, and – perhaps most importantly – a willingness to tell it to you straight when you get off track.

My grandfather and great-uncles trusted him implicitly. It's easy to see why. For Gerry, trust isn't something you ask for, it's something you earn. That belief didn't just fortify his personal relationships; it instructed his political instincts, where he has never lost sight of the fact that a voter's faith is sacred.

They Were My Friends is not just a memoir of a rich political career and a generational friendship – it is a roadmap for any public servant today, searching for a way forward in undoubtedly difficult political times.

In the pages to come, Gerry reminds us that it – always – starts at home.

Joseph P. Kennedy III
Member of Congress

Introduction

It was the silence – a profound, mournful, shared silence. My friend Teddy, the senior Senator from Massachusetts, died on August 25, 2009. On August 27, 2009, he was brought to the JFK Library where he was to lay in repose, flanked by a military honor guard as well as a civilian honor guard of family, friends and staff. Thousands of mourners silently waited in line to pass by his casket to pay their final respects. My wife, Marilyn, and I had been asked by his family to keep vigil in the first civilian honor guard. We sat by his casket for the first four hours of the public viewing. It was the silence that was overwhelming, palpable.

I was flooded with memories of my friend and our friendship of more than fifty years. I remembered – the first time we met at a luncheon at Locke Ober's, his debates against Edward McCormack and Mitt Romney, our conversations while he was in the hospital recovering from injuries from a plane crash, his hosting Thanksgiving for the Bolshoi Dance Company at his parents' home in Hyannis, searching for a site for the JFK Library and more, so much more. It was a great friendship; a friendship I will cherish forever; a friendship that changed my life.

People frequently ask me how I knew Ted. Actually, he was not the first Kennedy I knew or helped, nor the last. Initially, thanks to JFK's men from Charlestown – Frank Morrissey, Dave Powers, Billy Sutton and Bob Morey – I was introduced to JFK as a teenager. I was born and still live in Charlestown, a section of the City of Boston. Charlestown was a blue-collar neighborhood of hard working people, strong families and strong friendships. Later, I was enlisted to help Jack, Ted and Bobby politically. Each became my friend. It has been quite the journey. Here is my story.

Chapter 1

<u>The Beginning through High School</u>

I was born, raised, and still live in the same house in the Charlestown district of Boston. Many of the values I hold dear, such as thrift, integrity and independence, I inherited and acquired in my early years, and they continue to serve me well to this day. Two seminal events in my life can be traced to living at that Washington Street address in Charlestown. It was, I believe, because of air pollution in Charlestown that I and several of my neighbors were infected with tuberculosis. The second event occurred when I met a young candidate for Congress, John F. Kennedy, who stopped by my house during a parade pause to have a glass of lemonade.

At the time of my birth in 1928, Charlestown, Massachusetts, a district in the City of Boston, had a population of predominately working class Irish Catholics. It was a very densely populated area, with nearly twenty-five thousand people squeezed into approximately 1.3 square miles. The community is formed as a peninsula jutting into Boston Harbor across from downtown Boston. It was rimmed at that time with industrial manufacturing plants in the Navy Yard and an industrial district adjoining the Navy Yard. There is no longer any industrial manufacturing taking place in Charlestown. The Navy Yard has been converted into a new, mixed-use community featuring up-scale condominiums and apartments. The other industrial area has been converted to predominantly office use.

The Battle of Bunker Hill, one of the most significant battles of the early American Revolution, took place in Charlestown on June 17, 1775. Commemorating that famous battle each June 17th – or Bunker Hill Day – is an annual tradition in Charlestown. The highlight of the day is the Bunker Hill Day Parade. Its route includes Washington Street, passing directly in front of my house.

For the Bunker Hill Day Parade in 1946, I had invited two of my football teammates from Malden Catholic, Tan Doherty, an All-Star End, and Dan Bennett, an All-Star Halfback, to come over for the festivities. One of the first bands in that parade, from St. Mary's in Brookline, played "The Bells of St. Mary's." The band from St. Mary's received an enthusiastic reception on Washington Street since our local parish and school also was named St. Mary's.

The band was followed by a group of local fellows – Bob Morey, Frank Morrissey, Dave Powers and Bill Sutton. Charlestown was very much a small town. All of those men were well known and respected in the community. However, the man leading that group was not familiar. He wore a light tan suit and a soft hat. He was a young, skinny fellow; so skinny a mild wind could knock him over.

The parade came to a stop in front of my house. My father, as he did every year, had a pitcher of lemonade on the sidewalk, which he offered to the hot and tired marchers. Frank Morrissey, a good friend of my father's, brought the skinny fellow in the tan suit over for some lemonade. Morrissey introduced the man to my father: "This is John F. Kennedy, and he is running for Congress." My father called me over and introduced me to Mr. Kennedy, bragging that I had just been accepted to Harvard. JFK smiled and shook my hand to congratulate me. The parade then started up again and Morrissey and JFK rejoined their group and continued on their way.

This introduction, brief but monumental, would mark my first of many encounters with John F. Kennedy and the entire Kennedy family. At the time, I did not appreciate that this meeting would set the framework for my education, my career, and my life to follow.

Charlestown is a community that has a long history marked by interesting places, including John Harvard's original church, built in the late 1600s and the site of the first major battle of the American Revolution, the Battle of Bunker Hill. It is also home to the oldest ship in the U.S. Navy, the USS Constitution, berthed in the Navy Yard. Over the years, some of the town's most famous residents included Edward Everett, former governor and member of the United State Senate, and a major speaker at Gettysburg; Samuel F. B. Morse, inventor of the telegraph and Morse code; John Harvard, the namesake of Harvard University; John Boyle O'Reilly, poet, writer and journalist; and many others. For a time, Charlestown was dotted with a wide range of sturdy mansions and residences. Yet, in 1900 the elevated train system was built in the middle of Main Street, shadowing the town and creating an overhead eyesore. The "El" – for elevated train – blighted the area and Charlestown went into a decline. Wholesale abandonment of houses and buildings devastated the community.

Charlestown's population in the 1900s was primarily first generation Irish from County Donegal, Ireland. This odd settlement from the remote northwestern section of Ireland was not accidental. The new flock of immigrants was the result of a simple matter of transportation. In the port of Killybegs, Donegal, ships routinely sailed with boatloads of emigrants whose final destination was Charlestown. Their names, invariably, were Doherty, Brennan, McLaughlin and O'Neil. Nicknames prevailed in Charlestown to delineate the Edward Dohertys, John McLaughlins, Tom O'Neills, and Bill Brennans. Which Ed Doherty are you talking about? Big Ed? Little Ed? Short Ed?

My mother's family lived in the North End section of Boston, where they first immigrated in the late 1870s. My maternal grandfather, whose last name was Rowan, was elected to the state legislature. In the early 1900s, he and his family moved from the North End section of Boston across the bridge to Charlestown. He died young and left his wife Rosie (McLaughlin) with one child, my mother, Helen Frances Rowan. In 1918, she was a member of the first graduating class of St. Mary's Grammar School, where she was awarded the General Excellence Medal. She then went on to Mount St. Joseph Academy in Brighton, where she continued to excel in academics. She and my father, Edward Doherty, were married in 1922. Some believed she married below her station in life and that they were not a particularly good match for each other. Nevertheless, they had two children; my brother Edward, who was five years older than I – and me. We lived in the same home I live in today, but with a lot of relatives, cousins, uncles and friends.

I was born on April 6, 1928. Earlier that day, Good Friday, my mother was visiting the churches, as was customary. At about six o'clock, as she was going to St. Mary's Church in the North End, she was nuzzled by a horse, went into labor, and was rushed to Sunnyside Hospital in Somerville. While she was in labor she and the nurses talked about my name. One of the nurses suggested the name Gerard for St. Gerard, patron saint of mothers in labor. In my early years, the neighbors on the street who were not familiar with the name had difficulty pronouncing "Gerard." One neighbor called me Giraffe and another lady at the other end of the street called me Garage! It must have been something with the Donegal brogue, for 90 percent of my street came from Donegal.

My early education was a disaster. I had difficulty reading due to my dyslexia, which was not recognized until the third grade. Consequently, I was kept back in the third grade and was reluctantly promoted to the fourth grade. In the third grade, my problem displayed itself prominently one Valentine's Day. Sister Bernadette, my third-grade teacher, urged all the boys to write a Valentine note to one of the girls in the class. I wrote, "If you will be my concubine I will be your Valentine." Sister Bernadette did not approve and I, of course, didn't realize what I wrote.

That was the first year we had report cards. When I came home with disappointing marks, my mother was upset and would say in jest, "Maybe I took the wrong baby home." A motivating admonition I carried through my life and utilized whenever I was facing a difficult challenge. Even as dopey as everyone thought I was, I clearly understood what she meant. I was forced to wear glasses, which affected my coordination. Team sports evaded me. Girls were picked to play on softball teams before I was. I became sullen and shunned other kids. Hibernation was my solution. Living with all these social problems, I had one champion among my peers – my next door neighbor, Charlie Tryder. Charlie was one of eight children. His older brother, Paul, was my brother Ed's best friend. Charlie was my hero! He stood up for me time and time again.

Every other Saturday afternoon, Charlie and his younger sister, Dottie, and I would go to the movies. Because of my dyslexia, when the movie came on, Dottie would read the script on the screen to me. However, on one particular Saturday afternoon when the script came on the screen, like something out of a miracle, I could read it without Dottie's help! They were amazed. I was stunned! When I went home, I was so jubilant. My father, who always had been supportive of me, gave me the Boston Post and said, "Read it!" I read it quickly, without a problem. I remember it saying something about the Germans. My parents were both astounded.

In May of the fourth grade, final exams started. This series of exams were required by the Archdiocese of Boston to determine the academic readiness for promotion. The first exam was in music, which I took without any difficulty. It was followed by the Memorial Day holiday break. On my return to school that Monday, just before class began, Sister Edwardine motioned for me to come up to the desk. She asked me, "Where were you sitting when you took the exam?" She looked over to the spot and said, "No one over there could have helped you!" The next week we continued with final exams in History, Geography, English, etc. Four or five days later, my brother was asked to bring my mother to school for a meeting with Sister Edwardine. My brother never told me what that meeting was about until about a year later. He told me that Sister Edwardine gave my mother some good news, informing her that I would be promoted – on a trial basis – to fifth grade. She also divulged to my mother that I did well on all of the final exams, with scores in the mid-eighties. Sister Edwardine was extremely happy with my sudden scholastic achievement. If that miracle had not happened, I would have had to leave St. Mary's Grammar School and enroll in public school, which offered special education programs. Miracle or not, I did learn to really concentrate on what was being said in class so that reading was not my primary source of instruction.

The following September, I started fifth grade with Sister Mary Matthew, and on my first report card I had an average of eighty-four. My mother was ecstatic. In the sixth grade with Sister Rose, my first two report cards were in the low nineties. In March of my sixth grade, my mother was cooking a roast beef when she slipped on a piece of fat on the kitchen floor, spilling the entire pan of scalding hot grease on her chest. The burns were so bad she had to be rushed to the hospital in an ambulance. Not long after her return from the hospital she suffered a heart attack, which was most likely brought on by the burns she suffered, and passed away shortly after. I was only eleven years old. I was heartbroken. Up until then, my father had always deferred to my mother when it came to me. He had entrusted the raising of his sons to my mother. Now, he had the responsibility. We became very close, as he was interested and supportive in everything I did. He encouraged my friendship with Charlie Tryder who lived next door and, like all of his siblings, went to public school. Their father was a Protestant, which was unusual in our neighborhood. Mr. Tryder was in a high management position at H.P. Hood, the big milk distribution company in Charlestown. Eventually, all four Tryder boys worked there at one time.

During the summer prior to my starting the seventh grade, the neighborhood boys my age started a sandlot football team, the Washington Street AA "Washies." They wanted someone like Charlie Tryder to play on their team. He said he would only play if they let me play, too. They unenthusiastically agreed. So I became a football player. In practice I was inept, terrible, awkward and confused. Charlie recognized my difficulties. Surprisingly, I was okay at tackling, but most of the time I seemed confused and unfocused. After our group practice Charlie asked me to stay. He talked to me very seriously about my playing. He asked me about my vision. I told him I had a lazy left eye and had trouble with vision in that eye. He listened intently, then he said, "But your right eye is good?" I said, "Yes." In a very supportive, sincere voice he said, "You and I are going to try something and I think it will work out. We will practice a little before the rest of the team gets here."

The next day, about an hour before our group practices, Charlie and I met. "Let's try something." He spent about fifteen minutes running by me, and I would try to grab his shoulders. He ran by my left shoulder a couple of times. My effort to grab him was awkward and I missed him several times. When he ran by my right side I was almost perfect. Enthusiastically, he said, "I have an idea for you in practice today. Stand by me during practice." He told the team in a commanding tone, "For a little while, I want you to let Gerry play in the left position next to the center. We will run a couple kids past him first from right to left, like this." After about twenty minutes of running people from different directions, everyone grew impatient. When our formal practice concluded, Charlie had a couple of kids run by me, first from right to left and then from left to right. I was clearly much better watching people running right to left.

The next day Charlie talked to a couple of leading players and asked them to let me play left guard on the left of the center. Following Charlie's directions, I played much better. Our team played its first game against the Chestnut Street Eagles, and we won rather handedly. Our team was made up of mostly Irish names, but our two stars, along with Charlie Tryder, were Italian: Frank Riccardi and Basil Melo. They played in the backfield with Charlie. As the season progressed, we continued to win with great performances from Charlie, Basil and Frankie. Charlie was my best friend as well as a great runner for our team. However, he did have one weakness – he dislocated his shoulder in one game and thereafter it kept popping out, and it was my job to pop back in.

Our uniforms were made up of old clothes, double sweaters and several pairs of old pants. About half of us wore helmets, and those that did not wore stocking hats. My brother Ed, who was our coach, got together with Butch Morrison. Somehow, my brother found helmets for Charlie and me. We wore all sorts of jerseys and different shirts. Then we hit the jackpot. John "Hock" Horrigan, who lived at the end of the street, had an older sister, Helen, who worked in a sporting goods store. We were in luck. The sporting goods store made a mistake. They received an order from a prep school for red and blue jerseys. Instead, they turned out to be orange and black. That was a huge blunder for the prep school. The school refused them and would not pay for the company's mistake. Their misfortune was our gain. Helen had a proposal for her teenage brother who played on the "Washies." We could buy the orange and black jerseys for one dollar a piece. So we sold chances and raised enough money for twenty-seven jerseys.

Later in my life, I would learn another reason why Charlie was such a great friend. My father allowed me to invite boys and girls to my house for parties. The highlight of the party was playing "spin the bottle." Charlie was the best looking of the boys, so naturally all the girls wanted to kiss him. I was very shy and awkward at the time, so much to my delight when the girls kissed Charlie they also would kiss me. It was years before I was to discover the reason for my good fortune. Charlie had informed the girls that if they wanted to kiss him, they also had to kiss me. That is a good friend.

On Sundays, after early morning Mass, we had football. On December 7, 1941, the game was the "Washies" versus the "Parkies." In a big upset, the boys from Washington Street came out with a win. Heading home, we piled into my father's car singing, "We won because we won," over and over. As we pulled into the driveway still screeching, "We won because we won," my Uncle Skidder came running out of the house wearing only his undershirt and pants. He was shouting and waving his arms at us. Confused, we all quieted only to hear him shouting, "The Goddamn Japanese just bombed Pearl Harbor." There was silence, confusion. We scrambled out of the car half-dressed in our football uniforms, sullen, upset and bewildered. We all scattered in disbelief to our houses.

That evening all the church bells in Charlestown rang. Men and women flooded the streets, sobbing in disbelief. A neighbor came by to tell us there would be a prayer service at five o'clock at St. Mary's. All the other congregations, Protestant and Catholic, were gathering in their respective churches as well. The whole town prayed. We listened to President Franklin D. Roosevelt's radio address that evening. "A day that will go down in infamy…" A day I will never forget. The President said we were going to declare war on Japan, and one day later we did. Our lives changed. We changed.

Shortly thereafter, on December 8, 1941, Germany declared war on the United States. Two wars now. The following days were very hectic. During the day, we would practice for air raids. Mr. Goggin, a neighbor from down the street, told us to close our window shades to keep the light from coming through. My brother, Ed, was finishing up his first year at Boston College. As soon as he completed his spring semester, he joined the Air Force and went off to flight school in Smyrna, Tennessee.

My brother's friend, Dunny, who lived three doors down the street, had joined the state National Guard a year before. He joined because they would pay him twenty dollars a month to attend two drill training sessions. Once war was declared, his unit was activated. After two months of training, he was sent to the South Pacific, where he fought the Japanese for over two years. Dunny, one of many Charlestown men and boys who served in the South Pacific, contracted malaria, as did many others who served there. Another man from Charlestown, a priest, Father Brock, went to the South Pacific as a chaplain and stayed with the troops the entire time, particularly keeping an eye on the local boys from Charlestown. Meanwhile, my brother Ed failed his flight training test due to his poor depth perception. He then went to meteorology school before going to Europe, where he was stationed in England for over a year.

The war ended in 1945. The troops came home, but, sadly, not everyone. Our 1941 team, the "Washies," lost four boys to the war: Francis Kenny, a sailor, was lost in the South Pacific; Jack Crown was killed at the Battle of Bulge in 1944, as was Cluckie Mahegan, who came from the other side of Charlestown; and John Horrigan, center for the "Washies," was killed on the last day of the war.

In 1942, I entered Malden Catholic, a Catholic high school in Malden, operated by the Xaverian Brothers. Malden Catholic, about a half-hour street car ride from Charlestown, was respected for the quality of its education and strength of its athletics.

Academically, I had a very slow start in my freshman year, with my grades being average. But in my second year I maintained a B average. The main influence was one teacher, Brother Aubertus. In my first day of Latin class as a sophomore, the teacher, Brother Aubertus called on me. I stood up and responded, "I don't know the answer." Brother Aubertus walked down the aisle, grabbed my shoulders and said angrily, "Why don't you know?" I lamely said "I don't know." I had a bandaged, broken nose. He asked "What happen to your nose?" I said, "I broke it yesterday at football practice." He snarled, "I am going to call on you tomorrow and you had better have the answer or that nose will be on the back of your head." I quickly replied, "Yes, Brother." Over the next couple of weeks, he called on me for an answer every day, and I made sure I had the right answers to his questions. During the year, Brother Aubertus and I became good friends. Whenever he asked, I had the right answer. I did well in Latin thanks to his supervision.

Along with academics, sports also were very challenging at Malden Catholic, although I did not play football right away. When I entered Malden Catholic, I was still playing sandlot football with the "Washies," who won every game except two in the 1942 season. It was not until my junior year when I started playing football for Malden Catholic, as a substitute guard. In one of my first games against Arlington High School, a much bigger Class A team, I managed to block a kick for a touchdown. I landed awkwardly on my head and was knocked out cold. I was told the following conversation took place. The referee came up to me and asked, "How many fingers am I holding up?" I responded, "Where are you?" After a few minutes, I recovered and had to be helped off the field but was not allowed to go back into the game. My father and my aunt, along with my cousin and his wife, with whom we lived, were all there to witness the event. My aunt became so upset after seeing me knocked out on the field she almost fainted.

At home that night, my aunt was still very shaken up by the incident. Her attitude was subdued. My father was sullen and angry because of what had happened. We ate dinner pretty much in silence. I went to bed and woke up the next morning for eight o'clock mass at St. Mary's. When I got home from Mass, my father was still upset. Suddenly, he stood up and said, "That's it! Turn in your equipment. Everyone in the house is upset! No more football for you!" I was devastated.

The next day was Monday. Our team was still beat up from the Arlington Catholic game. At 1:30 p.m., the football coach called off practice. I went home and moped about. I was angry at the prospect of not playing football and turning in my equipment. For a distraction, I started to rummage around my house. By accident, I opened a sock drawer in my late mother's old bedroom and found some of my old playthings, including an unfinished, orange-knit doll's dress. I remembered making it in second grade. When we were summering in New Hampshire, my mother, after some insistence from me, taught me how to knit. The dress was six inches by four inches, with holes for arms. An hour later, my father came home. My father was an injured fireman who had a desk job at fire headquarters. Before his injury, he was very active. When he was stationed in East Boston he was a handball opponent of Joe Kennedy, President of the East Boston Savings Bank and father of the future President of the United States. As he came through the door, he saw me sitting there knitting. He was so angry at the sight of me knitting a doll's dress that he stormed upstairs, picked up my football jersey and the rest of my equipment and flung them down the stairs. He slammed the door and shouted, "Go ahead and kill yourself." Just like that, I was back on the team!

I played regularly in my junior year at Malden Catholic, which was a very good year for our team and me. We won the Catholic League Championship and six Malden Catholic players (including me) made the All-Star Team. During my senior year, I played as a left guard. My eye sight was frequently being questioned until one of my teammates, Joe Wilkins, explained to everyone: "Gerry does everything by memory. When he pulls left or right, he counts seven steps and then turns up field. After he turns up field it is all by touch. If the running back wants him to turn right he taps his right hip and vice versa, and if he wants to go straight, he put his hand up his ass." That seemed to satisfy everyone.

One memorable experience for me was the game we played at Cathedral in Springfield. It was a tough game. It was my first time backing up the line. Our coach, John Prior, tried this alignment for the first time. His scouting reports suggested that Cathedral had an explosive team and this alignment was our best defense. It was an up and down game. They ran and ran but never scored. It was a busy night for me. Tackle after tackle. The score, 21-0 Malden Catholic, did not reflect how physical the game was. The score was a result of our running back, Dan Bennett, who scored on long runs of 30, 50 and 80 yards. Bennett later went on to play for four years at Tufts College. After the game, the Cathedral coach, Billy Wise, who was a scout for Notre Dame, said he wanted to see both Dan Bennett and number 42 – me. We went to this room and he started to talk to us both. He asked us to stand up and walk around. He stopped, pointed at me and said, "Who are you?" I said, "You asked to see me." He responded, "Where is 42?" I said, "I am 42." He bluntly said, "You are really too small." He then dismissed me and continued to talk to Dan Bennett for a few minutes. He asked Bennett if he had any interest in Notre Dame, but Bennett said, "No!" This encounter was my day of recognition. My encounter with the Cathedral coach made me realize that I would soon have to start thinking seriously about possibly going on to college and playing football.

Late in the football season, we played one of our rivals, Keith Academy in Lowell, which was also a Xaverian-sponsored school. They were big and were having an outstanding year. Keith Academy had already beaten Lowell, Lawrence and Nashua and they were picked as favorites to beat us. The game itself was brutal. They were bigger and more talented. A good number of them went on to play college football. However, we ended up winning that game 14-6. We may have won the game but we were definitely the worse for wear. After the game, while we were getting changed, I could not get my football pants off. My right leg had swollen and ballooned up so badly they had to cut off the pant leg. I hobbled home that night. The next day was November 11, Armistice Day, a holiday.

Our coach, John Prior, had played football at Harvard and had arranged for me and a teammate to visit Harvard that following Monday. As the three of us toured the school and its grounds, I was still limping from Sunday's game. One of the Harvard faculty guides noticed and suggested we visit the athletic health office. A doctor there looked at my leg and said he could relieve the swelling by taping the leg, which he did. The swelling immediately contracted. After the tour, Coach Prior asked me if I had any interest in Harvard. I did.

Coach Prior arranged for me to take the college achievement test and aptitude exam. I took them in early December. The aptitude test was in the morning. In the afternoon, there were two achievement exams, one in Latin and the other in Physics. I passed both exams and did surprisingly well, so I applied to Harvard. In April, I was accepted.

My father, who left school in the third grade, was ecstatic. That night he met with his usual pals at Waldorf Cafeteria in Charlestown's City Square, and boasted to his friends about my acceptance. His friends asserted, "You're entitled to brag. John Harvard," (a founder of Harvard whose first church was established in Charlestown) "would approve." I graduated from Malden Catholic in May of 1946. At graduation, much to my surprise, I was selected as the Outstanding Student Athlete of the year.

Crossing the River to Harvard

In September 1946, I started at Harvard. The coach of the Harvard Freshman Football team, Coach Henry Lamar, gave me a tryout. He liked the way I tackled, but said my lack of weight was a problem. I only weighed about 160 pounds. He ultimately let me play defense only. However, he said he would use me backing up the line. I played about ten plays a game for three games: against Holy Cross College, Andover Academy and Exeter Academy. At that time, I was not feeling particularly great physically and decided it was best to give up on football. Little did I know that this was my first sign of TB. Instead, I enrolled in a lifesaving course to supplement my time and satisfied my requirements for a lifeguard certificate.

At the end of my first semester at Harvard, I attended a Friday night dance at our local YMCA in City Square. That night I met a tall, attractive girl named Margaret Crotty. We danced and I was smitten. She was a junior at Cathedral High School in the South End of Boston. A week or so later I called her to take her to the movies. She lived a couple of blocks away on Soley Street, near St. Mary's Church, with her mother, two younger sisters and a brother. Her mother had been widowed a few years and was wonderfully kind and well-liked. She was active in many church and youth activities. I dated Margaret up to the time when I was diagnosed with tuberculosis in 1948. When I went to upstate New York to be cured she wrote regularly. Twice she came to visit me during my lengthy hospital stay. When I came home in June of 1950, I continued to see her regularly. We were in love and excited about our future. While I was away, she finished her education at Regis College and taught at a public grammar school in Charlestown.

I went back to Harvard for two years to finish my education. We continued to date. The night after my graduation, I took Margaret out on a date. She said she had to tell me something. To my astonishment she told me that she was going into the convent with the Holy Cross Nuns at South Bend. Her announcement broke my heart. She did very well there and received a master's degree. She was selected to study for a doctorate and for some peculiar reason she was to go to Iran to study further. Margaret had some medical issues and needed some medical tests and exams. Unexpectedly, the doctors discovered she had a virulent form of cancer. She died three months later; she was not yet thirty!

While at Harvard, life was pretty uneventful when I wasn't playing football. I decided to join the Newman Club, a club for Catholic students at Harvard. One event I attended was a lecture by Father Leonard J. Feeney, S.J., head of the St. Benedict Center in Harvard Square. Father Feeney was later excommunicated from the Catholic Church for his anti-Semitic views. However, on the night of his lecture, one Harvard student stood up and angrily challenged Father Feeney and his views. His name, I would come to learn later, was Robert F. Kennedy.

In March 1948, during my sophomore year, I had a routine tuberculosis (TB) exam. A month later, I was informed by the Harvard Health Office that I had TB. I was sent to Harvard's infirmary for two weeks, where I took my final exams from my bed. After exams, it was decided that I would take time off from Harvard and go to a TB sanatorium in upstate New York for treatment. My father and I took a sleeper train; I took the upper berth. Perhaps that is why I could not sleep or perhaps it was because I did not know when – or if – I would be coming home. Those were daunting thoughts for a young man of twenty.

Detour to TB Sanatorium

On June 1, 1948, I was admitted to the Trudeau Sanatorium, a TB sanatorium in Saranac Lake, New York. The sanatorium, originally named the Adirondack Cottage Sanatorium, was founded by Dr. Edward Livingston Trudeau in 1885. At the time, the prevailing thought was that TB festered in heavily populated cities and towns that were industrialized and deemed unhealthy areas. It was thought that being in a clear, cold climate was the best environment to overcome TB. Soon Trudeau's treatment center became a hub for many TB patients.

Many of the doctors and the staff were TB survivors.

The cure at the Trudeau Sanatorium called for complete rest of the mind and body, to eat nourishing food and to have plenty of fresh air. The sanatorium was populated by cottages, each housing two to four patients. Dr. Trudeau believed the cottage atmosphere was most supportive of the basics of the cure – fresh air no matter the weather, highly nutritious food, a lot of rest before the introduction of carefully paced exercise and cultivating a positive attitude.

Upon registering at the Trudeau Sanatorium, each patient was given a small 24-page pamphlet, entitled, "Rules and Information for Patients." On page 24 was a signature requirement, whereby the patient agreed to abide by the rules and if there was any violation of the rules ignorance would not be a defense. The Rules stated that:

1. Patients are required to spend seven to ten hours a day in the open air. Provisions could be made to sleep in the open.
2. During the first week of treatment patients will have their temperature taken three times a day for seven days. Thereafter temperatures will be taken three times a day for two days each month.
3. The act of coughing should be suppressed as much as possible as this is one of the ways the tuberculosis is spread. Patients are required to purchase gauze at the Sanitarium shop to make handkerchiefs. Each day used handkerchiefs should be wrapped in paper for disposal. Each patient must have their own sputum cups which

are paper inside a cup frame. Each day the used spectrum cup is filled with sawdust, wrapped in paper for disposal.

4. Exercise is defined as walking or standing. Anything more strenuous can only be undertaken with permission. Each patient must keep a daily log of their exercise. An exercise clinic is held every Saturday at 11:00 a.m. The amount of exercise allowed is determined by the patient's exercise log.

5. All patients must be in bed by 9:00 p.m. and from 9:00 p.m. to 10:00 p.m. is quiet time. Lights out at 10:00 p.m.

6. Visits by other patients of different sexes is restricted to the front porches during the hours of 3:30 p.m. to 5:30 p.m. Visits inside the cottages by patients of different sexes is prohibited. A violation results in dismissal. Visits to any patient sick in bed is prohibited.

7. Use of alcohol stimulants is prohibited. Use of alcohol stimulants will result in dismissal.

8. Smoking prohibited inside the cottages. Smoking on the grounds is restricted to porches and permission must be obtained.

9. Patients are expected to take two warm baths a week. Each morning patients are expected to take a cold sponge bath to their waist. Patients are advised at night to take another cold sponge bath to their lower bodies. Teeth are to be brushed twice a day.

10. Meal schedule – breakfast 8:00 a.m. to 8:30 a.m.; dinner 1:00 p.m. to 1:30 p.m.; Supper 6:00 p.m. to 6:30 p.m. Permission is required for any deviation. Conversation between patients at meals about their disease and or

treatment is prohibited because it sometimes leads to depression.

11. Each patient will be notified by card when a chest x-ray is scheduled. Patients are also notified when urine and spectrum samples are required to be given to the lab.

12. Laundry is collected every Monday morning at 7:00 a.m.

13. All breakage and damage to the cottage is to be reported. Patients will be charged for all breakage. If breakage is not reported it shall be apportioned among the cottage residents.

14. A thermometer is provided each cottage and the residents are required to make sure the temperature does not rise above 72 degrees. When sleeping inside in cold weather the patients should cover the radiators with blankets to keep them from freezing.

15. Patients are expected to keep their cottages neat and clean and to make their beds each day before 9:00 a.m.

16. Between 2:00 and 3:30 p.m. is rest time in the cottages and there must be no conversation during that time.

17. All bills are payable in advance the first day of the month.

18. The library is available to all free of charge.

19. The Medical Director will make the recommendation to discharge.

20. On the anniversary of discharge the patient will send a report of health and work capability.

The Trudeau Sanatorium was a non-profit institution and it tried to keep the costs down. The costs for me were fifty dollars per week for room, board and medical supervision. Harvard contributed a little but my father, who was an inveterate "string saver," paid the bulk of the charges. It was an amazing feat for my father and it is a fact about my father that always amazed Ted Kennedy.

Switzerland, which was known for its cold, dry mountain climate, had a number of TB recuperative centers similar to the one opened by Dr. Trudeau. In fact, the author Robert Louis Stevenson had cured at centers in Switzerland. In 1887, he decided to leave Switzerland and sought curing elsewhere. Stevenson had heard of Dr. Trudeau's success working with TB patients at his sanatorium. So ultimately, he decided to go to Saranac Lake, where the climate was similar to that in Switzerland.

When he arrived, Stevenson remained active – skiing, hunting and fishing in the cool, crisp climate of the Adirondack area – until he broke his leg in an accident. With his broken leg, Stevenson was unable to move around; he became bed ridden. As fate would have it, Stevenson's physician was Dr. Trudeau. He noticed that Stevenson's condition seemed to get better with his reduced activity. As a result, Dr. Trudeau's treatment was modified to require rest in addition to exposure to clear, cold air.

Thus, the Trudeau Sanatorium standard treatment protocol was very well established when I arrived in 1948. A newly admitted patient, like me, was assigned to a cure cottage. Each cottage had a porch that remained exposed to the elements all year round. New patients were restricted to twenty-two hours of bed rest a day. Patients spent virtually all of their time on the open porches where each patient had a cure chair and a bed. I was assigned to Phoenix Cottage. A full complement in Phoenix Cottage was four patient roommates, with two patients sharing a porch.

Dr. Trudeau described a cottage in an annual report: "These structures are of yellow brick and stone, built in a most substantial manner, on plans which embrace all the features which long experience has shown best adapted to facilitate the treatment of patients by the open-air method in so rigorous a climate as that of the Adirondacks. They have been planned so that the beds may at will be pushed directly out on an open veranda, thus enabling the patients to continue the open-air treatment, even when confined to bed, and to sleep out at night on the sheltered veranda during the milder seasons, or when thought advisable."

As newcomers, we spent most of the twenty hours bundled up either in bed or in a cure chair. We slept on the porches in all seasons, including winter. At times, the temperature on the porch would fall to twenty-five below zero. At night from mid-November to early April the temperature on average was about zero degrees. A glass of water at our bedside was not permitted because it would freeze and break. However, that was not our major difficulty: It was being properly dressed to ward off the frigid temperatures in our exposed sleeping beds. When we had to heed the call of nature to go to the bathroom in the cottage, we had to shed our several layers of clothing that guarded us against outdoor exposure to the winter nights. Getting dressed and undressed was a major project because of our multitude of sets of silk pajama undergarments with custom heavy winter woolen outfits, topped with a couple of sets of sweaters. Our best aid was limiting the amount of water we drank after five o'clock. However, we all managed to survive the ordeal. Anecdotally, we would joke that summer came on the Fourth of July and winter came on the fifth.

Our meals were delivered by truck. At meal time, we would get out of bed and congregate around a dinner table located in the center of the cottage. Breakfast was pretty standard. Lunch was our main meal and generally we'd have a light meal for dinner.

The first six weeks were the worst for me. When you have TB, there is a natural anxiety that goes with the disease. However, when I first arrived my anxiety intensified, to the point where I was unable to hold down my food. What do you do all day when you are confined to a chair or a bed in a cottage in upstate New York? I was depressed, for I had no idea if I ever would leave the sanatorium alive. It was a frightening experience. My dear girlfriend, Margaret Crotty, helped me break the chain of anxiety, urging, "Do not lay around feeling sorry for yourself!" I had to do something. So I read books and newspapers to keep myself occupied. My anxiety abated. Because of my dyslexia it was difficult for me to read without a great deal of effort.

Usually after six weeks, your progress was reviewed. If, as expected, the patient improved, they were given a gradual increase in activities: Two weeks with fifteen minutes of exercise twice a day with the ultimate goal to receive an hour of daily activity. After completion of that course, the patient was given dinner privileges at a central eating facility. The average stay for most patients was about one year. Due to several minor relapses, I was there for two years.

Luckily, there was a breakthrough for me during this period. A new drug called streptomycin was administered to me for ninety days. I also received pneumothorax, which was a procedure that temporarily collapsed part of my right lung to reduce the level of breathing. With both treatments, I was able to go home in June of 1950, two years after my admittance. I felt like I was reborn. I was excited to see Margaret, my family and friends, and to continue my education at Harvard.

My experience at Saranac was more than just being treated for my TB. Patients at the sanatorium were very diverse. Initially, I was intimidated by how smart everyone else was. So, I listened and learned from them. Over the two years, I had about ten different cottage mates. They were stimulating, interesting, informative, considerate, and very unique companions. Herbert Brook was thirty-nine and a managing editor of the Yale University Press. Oddly enough, he had no middle name. Some of the older nurses could not understand how he was baptized as a Catholic without having a middle name. But, as we fondly knew him, he was well informed, pleasant and kind. Because of his job at Yale, he received newly released books, assorted periodicals and the Yale newspaper daily. He generously shared all these things.

Another porch mate was Carl Ernest Zimmer. He was a German Jew whose family escaped to Turkey because of Hitler's persecution of the Jews. He spoke Turkish, Italian, French, Spanish and English. He had been studying for his doctorate at the University of Chicago when he contracted TB. While he was at Trudeau, he taught himself Russian. He had a number of Russian books that he eventually passed on to me after he left, so I, too, taught myself Russian.

Tzuchaing Ho was from Hong Kong. He had been studying for his master's degree at Georgetown when he was stricken with TB. His father was head of the biggest bank in Hong Kong.

T.C., as he was called, was bright, funny, intelligent, quick, athletic and very good company.

All of these people were at Phoenix Cottage at different times, but individually and collectively they were stimulating companions. Being with them was a profound experience for which I am grateful. For me it was like being in college with a limitless library. Most were well-educated and relentless readers. One of the benefits provided by Trudeau was utilizing the resources of the varied but highly educated patient community. As part of their rehabilitation efforts, they encouraged patients who had special skills, either in the languages or the sciences, to offer their services to other patients. I became an avid reader due to a rehabilitating librarian. She tutored me and gave me an intensive reading course using the St. John's List of 100 Best Books. She tutored me twice a week, for which I gave her one dollar an hour.

I am not a "Pollyanna" about my experience during those two years. Our common bond was a disease. For the most part, patients had very positive attitudes about getting well and faced their illness with courage. One incident in particular comes to mind. There was a beautiful young woman from Puerto Rico curing at Saranac. She had a relapse requiring a serious operation. Minor procedures were done in the sanatorium, while more serious ones were done in the hospital in town. On the day she was to leave for the procedure, she came out of her room with a flourish, dressed in a traditional Flamenco dancer outfit, complete with a comb and a mantilla. As she went to the elevator, she danced for those of us who had gathered to wish her well. As the doors closed, she was still dancing. We found out later that she died not long after her procedure.

During my two years at Trudeau, I was enriched by my roommates at the Phoenix Cottage and by other patients. Even today, as I remember them fondly, I am stimulated and energized by my experience there. One particular memory comes to mind that really encapsulates the type of camaraderie that was present between all of the patients at Saranac. Over the Fourth of July, 1949, we were celebrating the holiday. At about eleven o'clock in the morning, there were ten of us gathered on the front porch of Phoenix Cottage. One of the men was from Reading, Massachusetts, and his name was O'Malley. He served in the army for three years and he began to reminisce about a certain day. He told the story of how five years earlier on the Fourth of July he was an infantryman in Belgium. He described his activities that day and how he was being shot at. One of our other roommates, Adolf Zimmermann, was an Austrian who had been conscripted into fighting for the Germans. He was fighting to hold on against an American advance, and was firing from an old barn roof. He and O'Malley started sharing more details of their action and they realized that Zimmerman was firing at O'Malley. It was an unbelievable coincidence. All of us were amazed at the coincidence. It was the highlight of us celebrating the Fourth of July and a memory that reoccurs every Fourth of July.

Returning to Harvard and Graduate School

In June of 1950, I left Saranac and was readmitted to Harvard as a part-time student. Normally, full time students would take four courses but I was restricted to three. I chose to major in Russian after having taught myself basic Russian at Saranac. I elected to take intensive Russian, which was a double-credit class, and Russian history. My intensive Russian required five days a week with one hour of instruction in the Russian language. My personal preparation in the language was based upon my Trudeau general familiarity with it, with my several months of personal study at Saranac. Study time was steadily required. My limited personal schedule gave me the opportunity to spend about three hours of regular intensive preparation each day. I worked very hard in the fall semester and I wound up with a Double A in my Intermediate Russian course and an A- in Early Russian History. For the spring semester, I followed the same course curriculum as the first semester with Contemporary Russian History.

In order to adjust for my first semester being limited to three courses rather than the normal course load of four courses, I attended summer school and took a course in European history. The following fall I took the normal requirements of four courses. History of the Middle European Ages, Shakespeare, and two Russian language courses. That year I made the Dean's List twice.

As graduation approached, I searched the job market very carefully and had a series of interviews arranged by the placement office at Harvard. When I got into the final stages of interviews, my draft status was raised and the prospective employers learned of my deferment because of my TB, and the fact I had pneumothorax administered every week. Any chance I had of employment vanished. By chance, I learned that the National Tuberculosis Association offered a scholarship to train students for careers in health administration with programs at Wayne State University in Detroit, Michigan. I filled out an application and I was accepted to start in September after my graduation from Harvard.

Prior to leaving for Wayne State in September of 1952, my father told me that John F. Kennedy was running for the Senate and that there was an event for him in Sullivan Square. My father and I went up to the event. We spoke to John F. Kennedy, who said he remembered me and wished me well in my endeavors at Wayne State.

At Wayne State, the curriculum was administered by the Maxwell School of Public Administration. The major course requirements were administered jointly with a group of graduate students in public administration. The whole program was overseen by Doctor Robert Mowitz, who had received his graduate degree from the Syracuse University School of Public Administration. In my group, there were six graduate students from an assortment of colleges: Alabama, University of Rhode Island, Buffalo University, Kent, and Pennsylvania State University. They were a varied and interesting group of people.

It was luxury living for me. I roomed on the graduate floor of the student center in a former hotel. I was downtown, two minutes from the facility that housed all of our classes, which were generally five days a week from nine o'clock to one o'clock. Mondays, Dr. Mowitz himself conducted the academic courses of administration. Tuesdays, he had guest lecturers who talked about their experience in various activities. For example, the mayor of Detroit appeared one day, and the general director of the National Geographic another. Their respective problems and solutions were outlined and discussed. These sessions were usually conducted over a friendly and informative lunch.

Most of the time, after the academic morning I would drop into the Catholic Newman Center, which was located on the edge of the campus. There I would chat with students who were local to Detroit or nearby locations. They were friendly, kind and interesting. Every week I had invitations for dinners at their respective homes. Of all the places I have lived, I found Detroit to be the friendliest and most genuinely interesting.

After my time at the center, I would go back to my room at about two-thirty and nap. Doctors had advised me to go slow and get plenty of rest. After my rest time, I would read for about an hour. At six or seven in the evening I would visit various group activities and socials throughout the dormitory building. Most of the functions had food, and that was my evening meal. Sometimes I would drop into the Newman Club for a while and visit. Friday evening the priests attached to the center would lecture on an interesting and timely subject matter for about an hour. After this talk there would be socializing for about an hour and half. Then I would go off to someone's home for a party. As a student at Wayne State, I found many happy times there and I remember them well.

Academically, it was interesting. Much of the reading I had done at Saranac was surprisingly helpful. My life as a student was great. Classes were interesting and informative. Doctor Mowitz picked on me to answer and comment on various matters. Most of the time he would almost snarl and call on me deviously and ask, "What does the gentleman from Harvard have to say on this matter?" He seemed to be surprised that my response most of the time was appropriate. The fall semester whizzed by quickly. In early December, he announced that our final exams would make up 65 percent of our credit courses. They would include matters from his course discussion and the presentations of our guest lecturers. The test would be given over a two-day period, consisting of three hours each day. Instead of being marked on a basis of 100, since so much material was covered, his marking would be based on 1,000. The exams were administered about ten days before the Christmas break. The results would be announced the day before we left for the holidays.

The fateful day for the results came. He seemed somewhat more somber than usual. His first comments indicated that everyone passed. He then digressed and announced that the top three students would have their choice of assignment to the various field training. He then emitted a sigh and said the highest grade went to Mr. Doherty. He smiled and said, "Doherty got a 963 as a mark." Over the eight years he had given these course examinations, it was the highest grade. He walked down the aisle, patted my back and said, "You surprised me!" Everyone clapped. I grinned. When I returned after the holiday break, Mr. Mowitz's whole attitude changed to one of friendliness. We became very good friends. He left Wayne State several years later and taught at Penn State. Twice he invited me there, when I was Democratic State Chairman in the early sixties, to lecture to his classes.

Drive to Training in California

In conjunction with my graduate requirements for my master's degree in health administration, I had to do a couple of things. It was required that I complete two months of active field training in a designated health agency. I was given the choice of doing my field training in Los Angeles or San Diego. I chose to do my active field training at the San Diego TB Association after my training in San Francisco. I went there in early June and had a delightful and helpful experience. However, the trip west from Detroit was a memorable one.

At the time I did not have a driver's license so my then girlfriend, Peg, who was a fellow graduate student and member of the Newman Club, would teach me how to drive on frequent trips to her summer home outside of Detroit. Peg was so nervous about my driving skills that her dress would be stuck with sweat to the back of the passenger seat. In Michigan, when taking your driver's test, you are accompanied by either a policeman or a fireman. When I went for my test, I lucked out and drew a firefighter. We conversed for a while and I mentioned to him how my father was a firefighter, and as a result he gave me a fairly easy driver's test and didn't give me anything difficult. And just like that I was a licensed driver. The first day of June 1953, I started my journey. At eight o'clock in the morning, Peg had arranged an outdoor stand-up breakfast at a small park near Wayne State as a going away celebration for me. There were about two dozen friends who showed up for my sendoff gathering. Peg had packed my few belongings in my six-week old used 1937 Ford, a selection that was aided by my mechanic friends at Wayne State. So, began my journey west.

Being a new driver in a brand new used car, I cautiously navigated through the streets of Detroit. Once outside of Detroit, I made good progress across Iowa into Nebraska, where I stopped for the night at the Shamrock Motel. I went into the lobby and I found out that the night rate was ten dollars. To me, that was too much. Just as I was going out back to my car, I heard someone yell that there was a tornado in the general vicinity. The radio on the counter was blazing with warnings. At that moment, I returned to the attendant at the motel counter and paid the ten dollars for the night. Dinner in my room was some of the canned fruit that my girlfriend had packed in the car, together with an assortment of cookies. The next day I crossed through Wyoming and made it across the desert through Utah into Nevada. A day later, after a long drive, I got into San Francisco and bedded down at the YMCA. There I stayed for about a week, during which I received orientation for my field training. At the end the week I departed for San Diego and was there for two months working for the San Diego TB and Health Association.

On my way to San Diego, I got extremely lost in Los Angeles. I pulled up to a cop standing in the middle of the street to ask for directions. He told me to back up out of the middle of the street into a spot on the side of the road and he would give me directions out of the city. Embarrassed, I muttered, "For my driver's test, I was never asked to back up." At first he was confused, then he stopped, looked at the Michigan license plate then looked at me. "You mean to tell me you drove all the way here from Michigan and you don't know how to back up?" The officer let out a sigh and blessed himself, "God help us!" I guess in my driver's test, the fireman and I got so deep into conversation that he forgot to test my backing-up skills. Eventually, I got some directions and was on my way to San Diego.

Luck was with me. San Diego turned out to be a marvelous choice. The director there was a fellow named John McCarthy. He was a great boss and wonderful friend. His wife, Grace, was originally from Boston's Brighton neighborhood and they had two children, ages eight and ten. They were wonderful to me. Grace, though her parish priest, found a very comfortable place for me to stay. I had a delightful accommodation with my own entrance, private bedroom and my own bathroom.

San Diego was a wonderful and happy experience. I worked for the local health agency. It was a marvelous summer. At the end of my field training, I drove back across the country to Boston and settled in with my brother Ed and his wife, Marguerite. My father remarried a very nice and kind woman, named Gert, and they lived in Quincy.

Returning Home: Job and Marriage

After being home for a month, I went to a dance at the Copley Square Hotel for Young Catholics. There I met my wife, Marilyn. I danced with her college roommate at first because Marilyn was dancing with someone else. I then danced with Marilyn. They were both from Our Lady of the Elms College in Chicopee. They had come to Boston to get a job. At the end of the evening I found out Marilyn was going to stay with an uncle in Newton, and she had to go there by public transportation. I offered to give her a ride to Newton.

I was not familiar with the roads to Newton and we ended up getting lost. After about an hour driving aimlessly around Newton, we found her uncle's home. I left her off, got her phone number and went home to Charlestown.

Not too long after my return from San Diego, I got a job as the director of the Greater New Bedford TB Association. It was housed about three miles from the center of New Bedford in a TB sanatorium where they provided me room and board. It was fine, but remote, so I would come home to Charlestown on weekends.

After the second weekend back in Charlestown, I called Marilyn. She was living then at the Frances Willard House, an accommodation for young working women, in the West End section of Boston. I called her and we went to a movie and had a pleasant time together. Almost every weekend that I came back from New Bedford we would go out together. Soon we fell in love and became engaged and shortly after that we were married – on September 10, 1954, in Pittsfield, Massachusetts, which had been her home.

After our marriage, we had an apartment on the fourth floor of 49 Monument Square in Charlestown. Marilyn continued to work in Boston at an advertising agency as I commuted back and forth to New Bedford. I would leave Charlestown early Monday for New Bedford, which was about an hour and a half away. I stayed in New Bedford Monday and Tuesday nights, came home on Wednesday evening, returned to New Bedford Thursday morning and came home Friday evening. Marilyn and I would have our weekends together. It was not a great arrangement but we survived. Other jobs, for either of us, were not easy to find.

After a couple of weeks staying at the sanatorium three nights a week, I began to hone contacts in New Bedford and I would join new friends in the evenings in downtown New Bedford. Surprisingly, there were a good number of college graduates who were located in the downtown area. For example, there was a young woman from Atlanta, Georgia, who was with the Girl Scouts. Also there was a young reporter at the New Bedford Times who had recently graduated from Pembroke College, an affiliate of Brown University. There were several newcomers with the textile companies that were located in New Bedford. Luckily, I met a couple of young people who were teachers. One young man I remember well was Jimmy Flanagan, a teacher whose family had a well-known candy distribution business. He knew everyone in the city. I became friendly with a young lawyer named Eddie Harrington, who later became Mayor of New Bedford. There was a fellow named Steve

Chiamp who had a lunch counter spot downtown, where in the morning I met with a lot of my contemporaries. It was an interesting group that intermingled socially.

After about a year staying at the New Bedford TB Association's Sanatorium, I took a room from a wonderful woman, Mrs. Pratt. She lived in a grand old home that was built by a whaling captain in the 1840s. In those days, New Bedford was a center for whaling. Mrs. Pratt provided me with lodging on the fourth floor of her home, in a sunny bedroom with an attached bathroom. We had breakfast every morning at eight o'clock. Mrs. Pratt's husband was a successful doctor for many years. They had three sons who went to Harvard, where they played football. She kept a very busy schedule with her charitable activities. Every week she spent three days as a volunteer at St. Luke's Hospital. It was always a surprise to witness her activities. The week before Thanksgiving, she organized a large group of singers from Yale. There were twenty-four in the glee group. The night of their performance it began to snow heavily. The singing group kept to their schedule and when they were finished the city was snowbound. At nine o'clock she brought the ensemble of twenty-four home to sleep. They did so on the floor and some in beds throughout the house. The entire episode did not faze her at all. For nearly two years, I had the wonderful experience of staying in her home four nights a week.

My obligations in my job were to raise money through the sale of Christmas Seals promoted by our local TB Association. That's how I earned my salary. Helping me was a great woman, Dorothy Aspin, who was energetic, smart and resourceful. There was a volunteer board of ten for whom I worked. The board included the local head of the health department, the pastor of one of the largest Catholic churches, a couple of lawyers and some businessmen. They were very supportive and helpful.

In the meantime, I would go back and forth to see Marilyn during the week and on weekends. During the fall, I coached a football team, but increasingly the schedule became a grind and it was not for Marilyn.

First Campaign

Then one weekend, on Saturday night, Marilyn and I went to a benefit dinner for St. Mary's Church. It was very well attended. It was filled with many of my contemporaries from grade school and my days of playing sandlot football. At our table were a lot of my old teammates from the "Washie" days. There was much talk about our local State Representative, Gerry Brennan, who had announced that he was going to become the Clerk of Court at our local courthouse. Speculation buzzed about who would run for his seat. It was the only elective position.

In 1954, I contemplated running for the open seat in the House of Representatives. People whom I knew from Charlestown encouraged me to run. Chris Callahan, who had already announced his candidacy for the seat, was the Grand Knight of the Charlestown Chapter of the Knights of Columbus and was also head of the local longshoreman union. He had a good following. He was a good athlete who had played football for a local team called the Crusaders. He and I clashed on the football field when we were younger. At a local event, various groups at different tables around the hall talked about me, whispering my credentials – Harvard graduate, played football for a local team, St. Mary's parish. Callahan heard the buzz. Standing at the bar, he laughed at my possible candidacy. He said, "If he is a Harvard man, he's probably an atheist and, on top of that, he speaks Russian." Then Callahan scoffed, "I'll bury him." I looked around at a nearby table filled with my "Washie" friends and said, "I am going to run for the House." My wife, Marilyn, was shocked, "If that's what you want to do, that's fine." The following day, I had to drive back to my job in New Bedford. On the way down, I covered all the various reasons why not to run. First off, I had a job forty-five miles away. I stayed in New Bedford Monday and Tuesday nights, came home to Charlestown on Wednesday night only to return to New Bedford Thursday night and come home late Friday afternoon for the weekend. That was the schedule that I had been following for more than a year. Many questioned, "With limited time, how could you possibly become a viable candidate?"

The first weekend I was home, I followed my brother Ed's advice and moved around the town. One of my first stops was the Knights of Columbus on High Street. There was a fellow sitting in the window. His name was Tom Carroll. His granddaughter and I had gone to St. Mary's School together. I sat down next to him. He quickly began to talk about my chances. He wished me luck but cautioned me about the difficult fight I was in. He then gave me a piece of advice, "Gerard, listen to me…go as far away from your house in the Valley, (a colloquial name for my neighborhood) and knock on all the doors there. Do it from now until September" (when the primary was being held). I looked puzzled. He said, "Listen. Be more 'Washie' than Harvard." I thanked him. I was somewhat shaken by his advice, but I was determined to follow it. His advice made sense to me.

I went home. At that time Marilyn and I were still living on the fourth floor of 49 Monument Square. I dressed in a clean shirt and sport jacket. I told her what I was doing and off I went to the area farthest from my home. I parked near a house in the Sullivan Square area and walked up to it with some trepidation. I knocked on the door. It quickly opened and an older gentleman in short sleeves said, "Can I help you?" I told him about my new-found candidacy. He politely listened and asked me for literature, of which I had none. He was kind and asked me to tell him about myself. I stuttered and stammered through my background. He smiled and said, "Sounds good. Come back with your literature and I will give it to my friends and neighbors." That afternoon I hit about twenty-five doors. Most of the people were home. Some were polite and listened; others were interested and urged me to come back when I had literature. I was encouraged by the general reception on my first campaign effort. No one slammed doors in my face or said they were too busy or "don't bother me."

That night Marilyn and I worked on my political cards. It told of my education – St. Mary's Elementary School, Malden Catholic High School, Harvard University – and of being a life-long resident of Washington Street (which was considered in the "Valley" section of Charlestown). Also listed on it were my affiliations: Knights of Columbus, member of Washington AA Football, Health Director in New Bedford, and St. Mary's Holy Name Parish along with my graduation photo from Harvard. I also included a proverb that was made famous by the religious leader, Father James Keller, and employed by John F. Kennedy: "It is better to light one candle than to curse the darkness."

People seemed very interested in the fact that I had TB. It came up as a result of my lack of military experience. I told them about my unpleasant experience with TB. Surprisingly, many had a family member with TB.

The field of candidates offered the election some options. There was Chris Callahan, President of the Longshoremen's Union who was very active in the union and from a long-tailed family; as well as Tony Scalli, an active businessman who owned a neighborhood market with an attached cafe. He was the unofficial patronage designee of Mayor Hynes. He was very well liked. Also in the field was a paraplegic who came from the top of Bunker Hill Street and married into a very political family. The other candidates were Bernie Kelly and Brad Brennan, whose mother-in-law owned a very popular tavern. Each had their own basic strength and their task was to multiply. Then there was me!

Charlestown was a political ward separated from the rest of Boston. My major strength was my name. There were over eighty Doherty families in town. Most had emigrated from Donegal. They called them "far downers," coined from the Gaelic, *fear donn*, which was used to describe individuals not from one's own country. Altogether there were about four thousand voters in Charlestown. Practically all of them were Irish and Democratic. From about the first of April, I campaigned every Saturday, Sunday, Wednesday and Friday nights. No one in the local political hierarchy paid much attention to my efforts, but I doggedly kept knocking on doors. For the longest time, my candidacy did not excite anyone.

One weekend morning in late April, I rang a bell on Monument Avenue, considered the well-off and affluent area of Charlestown. A man in his undershirt opened the door and pleasantly greeted me. He invited me in, offered me coffee or juice at his kitchen table. We began to talk about my candidacy. He politely interrupted me and said he knew who I was. He then proceeded to tell me about himself and his career in politics and how he served in the city council. It was an interesting story, and he could see that I enjoyed it. I told him a little about myself. He listened to my short presentation. When I was finished, he said in a kindly way, "You seem like a nice fellow, but you will not go very far because where you live in the Valley is the end of the world; out of the way, desolate and run down. No one succeeds from there." I was stunned, but I smiled and thanked him for his time. Showing me to the door, he said in a friendly way, "I hope for your sake I am wrong." Off I went, a little deflated but determined to keep knocking on doors. I was persistent. I thought to myself, "to hell with him."

Almost universally, people were kind and listened. Some had an unknown connection with my family. Some had gone to school with my mother, who had been deceased for twenty years. Some families with many kids knew me from St. Mary's School. Other than it being time consuming, hot, and tiring, it was not bad but it was hard work. Sometime in July, I knocked on a door on Walker Street, which was in the center of Charlestown. A pleasant housewife answered the door. She invited me in. Over coffee we had a pleasant chat. After about fifteen minutes, she walked me to her door and wished me luck. I thought I had her support. Shaking my hand, she said, "You are very nice." Then she shocked me and said, "I wish I could vote for you, but my husband, Wamo, is working very hard for Mr. Scalli." I was dismayed and stunned, but attempted to save face and said instinctively, "If you can't vote for me, you can pray for me." She smiled and wished me luck!

Obviously she told her husband Wamo, who was very active in Charlestown. Wamo knew a lot of people. He was entertaining and energetic. His conversation with many of his acquaintances would be loaded with cute parables and ridiculous stories. He told one of his cohorts a story that suggested that if I ran and got elected, I probably wouldn't live through my term, insinuating I was sick with TB again. Wamo suggested, "No, Doherty will strangle on his rosary beads." One of Wamo's cutting great lines, in jest, "Ya know, on Sunday Gerry goes to the seven o'clock Mass at St. Mary's, eight o'clock at St. Francis, and nine o'clock at St. Catherine's, and receives communion at all three."

Even after that, I found a fairly good amount of support from former football opponents. Many of them worked hard as longshoremen. They were almost entirely big and athletic. When they would put Doherty stickers on their cars or houses, some wise guy would come along and tell them to take the Doherty signs down. My friends would assure me, "Don't worry Gerry! Remember, stickers don't vote. People do."

In August, a trickle of calls of support to my house began to swell. More and more of my schoolboy counterparts offered help. On the other side, Mayor John Hynes's organization began to promote their candidate, Tony Scalli. Early in September there were several rallies for candidates in various districts. Politics was a sport in Charlestown. At one of the more memorable rallies, one of the candidates, Joe Murphy, got up and yelled out: "Doherty lives on the fourth floor on Monument Square and, if elected, if you had a problem, you will have to climb four flights to see him and probably die of heart failure before you got up there." My father jumped up and said, "Sit down, and keep quiet."

Although I still continued working in New Bedford, every chance I could get I campaigned in Charlestown. One of my advisors was a lady, May Quigley. "Gerry, work on anything and everything in the community, but don't be the head of anything. Be a worker. Just ask, 'How can I help?'" Then she told me the parable of square tables and round tables for events. "Help, but don't be in charge of anything." Time went by, and any function that I could help at I became involved as a worker. My brother and I even played dramatic roles in two minstrel shows. One a pantomime of "This Is Your Life," and the other a comedy about Ireland. One of my critics likened me to a bad penny that always showed up.

The week before the election, we had a hurricane. My door-to-door campaign intensified. My momentum was surging. However, I lost two days because of the storm. I had a good number of volunteers. Before I began to run, I did not know most of them. Mayor Hynes started flooding the area for my opponent Scalli. City workers were encouraged to vote for Scalli. After a tumultuous day of campaigning, when the voting ended at eight o'clock, I had lost to Scalli by only forty-four votes. The other candidates fell behind a considerable amount. There were mixed reactions. Marilyn and I were disappointed, but not devastated. The general feeling throughout the community was surprise, but it bode well for the future.

Gerard F. Doherty

Chapter 2

First Campaign Win

The first time I ran was partially on a dare. The second time was different. In January of 1956, I started to campaign again against Tony Scalli. Campaigning was easier now that I had some experience. The 1954 campaign provided me a road map. First, my wife Marilyn and I went through the voter lists for all the precincts, highlighting families with three or more voters. We also compiled a list of all the Doherty families in the town – there were a lot of them – eighty-nine in number! Then we made a list of the homes and families that I had visited during my last campaign. By this time, I had the benefit of dedicated friends and my campaign committee, whom I endearingly re-ferred to as my campaign managers. In April, I sent thank you notes to all the households that had supported me in my first campaign, advising them that I was going to run again.

Then I began visiting voters, again asking for their support and listening to their comments and concerns. I met many new people. One of the most memorable was a fellow named Frank O'Keefe. He turned out to be one of my most helpful support-ers. In March, I knocked on his door on Putnam Street near the Navy Yard. His wife answered. She was very friendly; she re-membered me from St. Mary's and my last campaign. She in-vited me in and introduced me to her husband, Frank. Initially,

Frank was very shy. However, he soon warmed up and became very talkative. He offered to help. He said he was not comfortable ringing door bells, but offered to help by delivering campaign materials. Frank then told me that he was a camera buff and even showed me his dark room, which was surprisingly well-equipped. He offered to take photographs of any group or at any event, which we could then send to the local newspaper. I thanked him and said I would be in touch.

In Charlestown, the "EL" was the elevated street car line that ran from Boston through Charlestown, along Main Street to Everett, the next town. The EL was ugly and noisy and a blight, which decimated Charlestown. It was finally torn down in 1975.

Shortly after my visit with Frank O'Keefe, I was riding the EL home from downtown when I ran into an old friend from Harvard, George Kevarian, who later went on be the Speaker of the Massachusetts House of Representatives. George had been a year behind me at Harvard when I returned after my bout with TB. We would regularly eat together at the student center and became good friends. George had recently been elected an alderman in Everett. We chatted about our campaigns. George mentioned that he had used pictures of significant buildings in the various neighborhoods of Everett in his campaign literature, which was mailed to Everett voters. He says he used the pictures to show that he was connected to the community. George had always been a very clever and resourceful fellow. I immediately thought of Frank O'Keefe and his camera. As soon as I got home, I called Frank to ask him if we could do something similar for my campaign. We settled on his taking photographs of neighborhood landmarks such as the Bunker Hill Monument,

Old Ironsides, the courthouse, churches and other significant buildings or sites.

Three weeks later, Frank called me to say that he had some ideas about how we could use his photographs. When we met, Frank showed me an array of photographs he had taken of residences in town. One depicted two attached three-deckers. There were some twelve to sixteen voters living in those houses. Another depicted a three family which would have about fourteen voters. We decided to get more photographs. A week later, Frank brought more photographs of houses, some single-family houses, others two and three families. Except for the public housing complex, approximately 75 percent of the town consisted of two and three deckers. The rest were single family homes. Frank estimated that, excluding the housing project, he could photograph the homes of about 70 percent of voters. He would take the photographs; I would buy the film. For two or three days, he experimented with various approaches in areas where I thought my vote could grow. Within six weeks, Frank had methodically photographed homes in every precinct.

In the meantime, I kept visiting voters. Usually, I would stop when it got dark, trying to make the last visit of the day a visit with a friend who would not mind my ringing his bell. We would talk about the neighbors, who worked where, and who had a lot of relatives in town. At first, I would visit some fifteen houses a day. As the days got longer, I visited twenty homes per day. Over an eight-month period, I visited approximately twenty-four hundred homes in Charlestown.

During these visits, I would talk with the voters, listen to their suggestions and concerns and ask for their support. As I left each visit, instead of asking people to pray for me as I had during my first campaign, I would say, "If you can't vote for me, then please vote to re-elect Sheriff Fred Sullivan." Sullivan was from Charlestown, went to St. Mary's Grammar School, Boston Latin School and Harvard, and served as a colonel in the army in World War II. Sullivan had been appointed by former Senator Joe White from West Roxbury. For reasons unknown to me, Fred Sullivan and Senator White had a serious falling out. Senator White's son, Kevin White, later became Secretary of State and Mayor of Boston, and was married to Kathryn Galvin of Charlestown, the daughter of former Boston City Council President Bill Galvin. Kevin White ran against Fred Sullivan in the election for sheriff in 1956. The White-Sullivan contest was bitterly acrimonious and very close.

Frank finally completed photographing the homes in Charlestown. The next step was more challenging. We had to match the appropriate photograph to send to the right household. My sister-in-law, Marguerite, volunteered to take on this particularly daunting task. Amazingly, she and a group of her friends methodically assigned each photograph to a corresponding household within three weeks. Marguerite and her friends addressed and stamped more than 2,200 envelopes. In each envelope, there was a cutout of one of Frank's photographs with the caption: *"Recognize this? Of course, you do! Gerard Doherty does too. He has walked your streets and visited your homes to tell you about his candidacy."* The photograph campaign brochures were mailed out two weeks before the election.

The impact of the mailing was immediate and overwhelming. People loved it. The whole town buzzed about it. More than two dozen people who received the mailing called to ask for extra copies so that they could send the photograph to their sons in the military or some other relative. The photographs gave my candidacy a huge surge in momentum. Of course, my opponent and his supporters were dispirited. The project was a huge success.

Election Day was tremendous. My brother Ed, my campaign manager, recruited volunteers to work the polls. We had some 200 people show up to help, including many of my old sand-lot football opponents. They worked the polls in areas where they lived or where our campaign was weak. Workers for my opponent taunted some of them, asking how much I was paying them to work the polls. "Nothing," they said in more colorful language. Later that day, the results were in. Of the seven precincts, I carried four. Our victory party started with a motorcade of thirty cars riding through the town with blaring horns and their occupants rejoicing, "We won because we won" over and over. Six weeks later, in the final election, I defeated my Republican opponent by four thousand votes.

We celebrated with friends and supporters at my home. Having urged Charlestown voters to vote for Fred Sullivan for Sheriff, I was interested in the results of the Sullivan-White race. Early on, White had been leading. However, when the final vote came in, Sullivan had been re-elected. Fred Sullivan personally called to thank me. His tremendous vote in Charlestown had been crucial to his re-election. Many of our mutual friends told me how angry Kevin White was with me for supporting Sullivan and that he would never forgive me. He never did!

Shortly after the election, I left my job in New Bedford and Marilyn and I moved into my old homestead, on Washington Street in Charlestown. My brother and sister-in-law had a baby and moved to Beverly, Massachusetts, leaving our family home empty.

January 4, 1957, was one of the most memorable days of my life. On that day, I was sworn in as the duly elected member of the Massachusetts House of Representatives, representing the Second Suffolk District, Charlestown. That morning, family and friends gathered at our house before going to the State House for my swearing-in. My father was the first to arrive, and motioned for me to join him in the living room. Marilyn and I were in the process of doing the house over so there was no furniture in there. We each brought a chair from the kitchen and sat down facing each other. My father, a retired fireman, was then sixty-five years old. He looked at me and spoke very seriously. "You have had a good education. You're smart, thanks to your schooling at Malden Catholic and Harvard. But there are some things they don't teach you in school. First, remember where you came from and that the people of Charlestown come first. Second, remember, always keep your word but don't give it too freely. Third, for your departed mother's sake, vote to legalize Beano; she loved that game. And lastly, never be alone in a room with a Republican. He will cut your heart out, and tell you it was to help with your ventilation. Remember to vote Democratic and you won't get in trouble."

Later that morning, we all went to the State House where Marilyn, my father, my brother and many family and friends witnessed my swearing-in at the convocation of the legislature. After the ceremony, I was introduced to several novice representatives, like me: Bob Quinn from Dorchester who later became Speaker, George Kenneally from Dorchester, John Linehan from Mission Hill, and George O'Shea from Lynn. They became my closest friends. Some three days later, I received my assignment for the Committee on Education. My new friend George Kenneally received the same assignment. At the time, the House of Representatives was controlled by the Democrats, but just barely. Total membership of the body was two hundred and forty. Mike Skerry from Medford was the Speaker, John Thompson from Ludlow was Majority Leader and Christian Herter, a Republican, was our Governor.

Law School and My Years in the Legislature

On the second week of the session, I showed up at the meeting for the Committee on Education, which was located way back on the fourth floor of the State House. When I entered the room, there was an older man already seated at the long-extended table. We exchanged greetings. He introduced himself as Cornelius Desmond of Lowell, Chairman of the House on the Committee on Education. I introduced myself, "I am Gerard Doherty of Charlestown." We exchanged some unimportant pleasantries. In a commanding voice, Desmond then said, "You are a lawyer, aren't you?" I quickly responded, "No." He queried, "Are you intending to become one?" Confused by his question, I said, "No," and blurted out that I was a Russian scholar. He exclaimed, "You are what?" I sheepishly repeated that I had studied Russian at Harvard. Desmond then said, "You are not a lawyer. You should be!"

Then Desmond looked at the clock and said, "Come on." I got up and followed him out the back door of the State House across the street to the administration building of Suffolk Law School. Desmond asked to see Miss McNamara. The woman at the front desk turned and went into an adjourning office. She returned and said, "Miss McNamara will see you now." We were ushered into a modest office where an older woman, Miss

McNamara, greeted Desmond. Desmond then introduced me and told her that I wanted to go to law school. Miss McNamara asked about my education and background. She then handed me a packet of materials and said, "Fill out the questionnaire and return it and you will start right away." Just like that, I was enrolled in law school.

Throughout my time in the legislature, I made many acquaintances, some of whom were less conventional than Desmond. Bill Wall, for example, was first the representative for Lawrence who later became a state senator. There were many stories about him. However, I recall only the best of them. He rightly loved and deserved the title of public servant. One day, he was struggling up the stairs of the State House with a new baby carriage. When I asked him about it, he told me that a constituent had called him the night before and asked if he could do her a favor. He assured her that he would try. She said there was a sale on baby carriages at Jordan Marsh, and asked if he could pick one up for her and that she would pay him when he came back to Lawrence with it. That is what he did. That was just the type of guy Bill was.

There was another unforgettable story about him as a Fourth-Degree Knight of Columbus. He was attending an affair, resplendent in his Knights of Columbus cape and his ceremonial hat. A woman tracked him down by phone. She told him about a family dispute, and how her brother got very emotional, yelling and screaming. The police came and brought him to the Danvers State Hospital for emotionally disturbed individuals. She pleaded with Senator Wall to get her brother out of the asylum. Still in his Fourth-Degree Knights of Columbus ensemble, with the ceremonial hat and scarlet cape, he rushed to the hospital on his mission of mercy. The guards greeted him in his unusual ensemble. They figured he was a disturbed sick person and locked him up. When he explained himself, they eventually let him go free.

However, one of his most unusual acts was during a session in the Senate. There was a long-fought tax bill realignment that was stuck for passage. The vote was tied. Because of the importance of the bill, the Senate Chamber was locked and secured by the court officers to make sure all the senators had been accounted for. Senate President Kevin Harrington of Salem had already cast his vote in favor of the tax. After half-an-hour of counting and recounting members, Senator Wall was the only senator missing. By coincidence, the urge of nature forced Kevin Harrington to go to the men's room. As he was coming out, he noticed that there was an out-of-order sign on one of the closed stalls. The six-foot-seven Senate president peeked over the stall to see Bill Wall hiding there, fully clothed. At the command of the Senate president, Senator Wall got out of the stall, returned to the Senate Chamber and voted for the bill. The bill passed.

Like Bill Wall and Desmond, there were many people in the legislature whom I could turn to for advice or counsel. One was a brilliant Paulist priest, Father Robert Quinn, C.S.P. In the 1960s, Father Quinn, a native of Medford, was assigned to the Paulist Center, a Catholic chapel on Park Street, steps away from the State House. In the 1960s, the Paulist Center became very popular. These were years of change in the church. Father Quinn was very much attuned to the changes stemming from Vatican II, bringing Church leaders and theologians from around the world to Boston to speak at his Christian Culture Series. There was a tremendous upheaval.

In 1968, Father Quinn became the Curator of the Paulist Center. At the time, there were four assistant Paulist priests assigned there. By the end of 1968, all four had left to marry. As the senior priest, Father Quinn was battered, blamed and accused of being irresponsible. Thus, his order forced him to leave his position at the center. In my opinion, he was unfairly accused and treated. I was not alone in this. Throughout his many years at the center, Father Quinn had developed and enjoyed the support of many in the congregation and beyond. Many parishioners were upset and angry at the treatment afforded to him. He endured this time of challenge with strength and dignity. Ultimately, he remained a Paulist and was allowed him to remain in Boston and to assist at St. Joseph's Church in the West End of Boston.

Like Charlestown, the West End had been a thickly populated residential neighborhood. Urban renewal changed the character of the area radically. New development and the expansion of the Massachusetts General Hospital during the 1950s and 1960s had an adverse impact on St. Joseph's parish. The number of parishioners had dwindled. When Father Quinn arrived, the parish was in decline. Father Quinn attracted many new parishioners.

Father Quinn also helped Monsignor George Kerr, who was Chaplin at the Massachusetts State House of Representatives. In 1981, Father Quinn succeeded Monsignor Kerr as chaplain.

Father Quinn lived near the State House on Bowdoin Street. He would regularly invite friends to his apartment for breakfast, during which they would discuss current events and important issues on a variety of topics, such as public education, health care, housing, courts and law enforcement. People spoke

– and sometimes argued – freely, never worrying that they might read what was said in the newspaper. The breakfasts were simple; the discussions profound.

In 1971, Father Quinn formed The Park Street Corporation, a nonprofit educational corporation through which he continued the breakfast meetings. The breakfasts attracted local leaders in business, education, law and government. The board of directors of The Park Street Corporation included many prominent leaders, including John Cullinane, a successful software developer; John and Leo Corcoran, housing developers; Edward Masterman, a lawyer; Thomas Flatley, a housing and commercial developer; Rudolph Pierce, a lawyer; Bill White, head of the Mass Housing Agency; Gerard Mulligan, a Massachusetts Banking Commissioner and, later, bank owner; Herbert Hoffman, a Boston businessman; City Councilor Tom Menino, who later became Mayor of Boston; and many others. The first time that Tom Menino came, someone said facetiously that, as the new guy, he had to bring the donuts. For the next two years, every time he came, Tommy brought the donuts.

For some six years, Father Quinn would also host larger breakfasts in various hotels with a guest speaker addressing timely civic and political topics. These gatherings attracted from 350 to 400 attendees. Tickets were usually one hundred dollars, which not only supported The Park Street Corporation but also funded donations to various social groups and charities around Boston.

Father Quinn was chaplain of the House of Representatives for thirty years. He helped many of the respective members and their constituents with advice, counsel and problem solving. He also was very active serving on various advisory committees, including the Governor's Advisory Committee for Housing and

Community Development, the Advisory Committee for the Boston Housing Authority, advisory committees for the City Assessor, and the Mass Convention Center Authority. On October 31, 2015, this wonderful priest passed away. His kindness and counsel played a very significant role to so many.

Another friend and mentor with whom I had the pleasure of working with during my time in the legislature was Sheriff Fred Sullivan. I had supported him in his 1956 re-election campaign. Over the years, Sheriff Sullivan and his wife, Muriel, became very close friends to me and Marilyn.

In February of 1957, Sullivan asked if I could drop by his office to talk. During our meeting, he was very sentimental and said some nice things about our growing friendship. Then he said, "This is going to be my last term. It will be over in six years. I like the people I hired and I want to protect them in the future. For that reason, I would like you to succeed me. I want you to become my deputy and will groom you as my successor. You can keep your House seat until the end of the term. If you agree, you can start in a week. Your salary will be two hundred and fifty dollars a week while you learn the various aspects of the job. Talk to your wife and let me know as soon as possible." I was flattered and surprised. All I could do was thank him for his kind offer. The only way I could respond was, "I will get back to you in a couple of days." I went home and talked to Marilyn. She was obviously surprised, "What do you think?" I thought and reflected about what the added income would mean – perhaps a new parlor set, vacations, clothes and lots of other things we did not have. The next day, I got back to the sheriff. I thanked him for his thoughtfulness and agreed to take the job. The following week I was installed as deputy sheriff and began my new job.

As deputy sheriff, one of my main jobs was to deliver court summons. One thing I learned from Sheriff Sullivan was that, when delivering summons, you should always walk up to the person, shake their hand with your right hand and hand them the summons with your left. That way they could not punch you with their right.

My days became very busy – law school, legislative duties, attending sessions of the legislature and my sheriff office duties. It was just too much. Taking the sheriff's job, I would not have to run for re-election. After three months of trying to do everything, I began to have doubts. The work at the sheriff's office was very somber and tedious. I was not happy. I enjoyed politics and constituent services much more.

Serving My District and Re-election

Meanwhile, word spread in Charlestown. It soon became well known that I would give up my seat in the House of Representatives to become full-time deputy sheriff. Many of my friends were sad and disappointed and told me so. Constituents and supporters also expressed their disappointment. Increasingly, I became uneasy about my decision of withdrawing from community activities. Marilyn noticed my uneasiness. One night at a late dinner, she said to me "What's bothering you? It's the sheriff's job, isn't it?" I responded a glum, "Yes." "Do you want to give it up and stay in the House of Representatives?" I said, "Yes!" The next day, I went to see the sheriff to thank him for his kindness and to tell him it was not a good fit for me or for him. Unfortunately, the sheriff had been hospitalized with pneumonia the night of my decision. In consideration of his ill health, I decided to wait to tell him my decision. Out of respect for him, it was important that I not tell anyone else about my decision. He deserved to be the first to hear of it from me.

It was about two weeks before he was well enough for visitors. Finally, it was an opportune time to see him. The visit was late one afternoon. Appropriately, his wife Muriel, who had been very kind to me, was with him. They both greeted me affectionately. I was very nervous and embarrassed but I stammered out my plans and decision. Muriel patted my hand and said, "You were a great friend to Fred when he needed you. You were there. We will miss you but you are a friend, and a friend will always be a friend." I was overcome by mixed emotions: sadness, embarrassment and amazement, without words. The sheriff, in bed, put his hand out, grabbed my hand, and said, "You were with me when I needed a friend. Good luck." I was speechless. I got up to leave and said, "I'll always be around to help. Thank you for everything." When I describe the meeting to Marilyn, she cried. I think I did too. My only thought was "they are two great people."

It was now mid-June of 1957. The political season had begun without me. Charlestown was loaded with Scalli signs and bumper stickers. I had to get into the race and quickly announce that I would run for re-election. Tony Scalli was well-liked. When it appeared I would not be running, Scalli had done a lot of work. Some of his more aggressive supporters were angry and they showed it.

They were not the only ones upset with me. Good friends were concerned. It was late and some of my friends had decided to support Scalli this time; they were not going to change. Many close friends were irritated that I waited so long; others thought

I was inconsiderate; others were puzzled about my behavior. The rumor mill worked overtime. Stories were circulated that I did not leave the sheriff's office under good terms and that I was fired for incompetence. My late entry into the race was compounded by the fact that Mayor Hynes's people in Charlestown had become much more active for Scalli. This was the fight of my political life.

The first order of business was to file my candidacy papers with the required number of signatures. That was complicated by my late entry. Some of my friends who had already signed Scalli's papers could not sign mine. Gathering signatures was going to be complicated. However, I knew what I had to do, so I had better get to it.

The base of my strength had melted away in some places. After some reflection and conversations with several of my friends, it was almost the universal feeling that I follow the plan that got me elected previously, with a few minor exceptions. They told me that I had won my first election because of my door-to-door campaigning. That was my strength. Repeat it! Some had reservations that I could not easily call on people. My good friends said, "The homes you will be going to will either have a request or a complaint. 'You did not get my son a job,' or 'You didn't get a pothole in front of my house fixed.' Some will crucify you. Others will want to talk to you for hours. Your pace from last time will be limited." My adversaries' comments were upsetting but I agreed to try the door-to-door for a while and see how it went. My friends encouraged me, "You must be here full time now! Last election much of your time was spent in New Bedford. Gerry, try it for a week and see how you think it is working out."

The next day I went door-to-door on Sever Street, near Sullivan Square. With some uneasiness, I went to the first door and knocked. The door opened. It was a middle-aged woman who smiled and said, "I knew you would be around soon." She called her husband to join us. We chatted for a while. He said, "Don't hold him up. Gerry has a lot of houses to visit. Good luck!" Off I went. Repeatedly, I got a similar reaction from voters in that area. I got a lot of, "You are the only one who ever comes to visit," or "My son will be sorry he missed you." At the end of the day I hit about thirty houses, all of which were filled with supporters, and some who even wanted signs. That was my general reception. It was me coming to see them…no one else was doing that!

One Saturday morning, I was still working the Old Sullivan Square area. On its edge, there was a cluster of triple deckers, each of which had three units. I knocked on the first door. I waited a few minutes before a middle-age woman opened the door. She seemed confused and gestured for me to wait. She called into the apartment and quickly a middle-aged man came out. He looked puzzled. I then started to introduce myself. He spoke to his companion in a foreign accent and then to me. I tried responding in Russian. He replied, "No, I am Polish."

We then conversed in English about the purpose for the visit. He gestured for me to stop. He turned to the woman telling her to get somebody else. She pounded up the stairs, calling out in Polish. There were other voices. In minutes, there were about six people crowded into the first-floor hallway. The man uttered a few sentences in Polish and then in English and the group listened intently. He explained to them my story and why I was there. When he finished, they applauded. The first-floor leader brought me to the next two houses. My new friend repeated my story to his neighbors. They all applauded. He told me that they all liked my story. He also volunteered that his neighbors were all citizens and were registered to vote. I was their man! They applauded. Some even spoke Russian, wishing me luck. Off I went enthused by my new-found support. From there, I had a very busy day, finishing about five hours later.

My most memorable experience in my door-to-door campaigning took place when I ventured into a small area of Charlestown that I had not visited. As I approached one house, I was surprised to see a Doherty sign in the window. I rang the bell and a woman in her forties opened the door and invited me in. She smiled as she said, "You don't member me, do you?" I said, "No, I don't," whereupon she jogged my memory with her name, Jody, and the phrase "spin the bottle." She then told me the story behind all the kisses that I had received. They were not because of my good looks, as I had thought, but because of my friendship with my best friend Charlie. We both had a good laugh and I admitted to being a little deflated. The truth does that sometimes.

The ensuing weeks were encouraging. A surprising number of people knew who I was and were generally supportive of my voting record. The pace of my house visits picked up. Despite seeing a lot of Scalli signs, my reception was good. I was surprised by the number of strangers who supported me. Some guys made comments about playing football against me. They good-naturedly said they would not hold that against me. During my street-by-street effort, I also met a great number of Dohertys. If they weren't Dohertys, they had Donegal names like McLaughlin, O'Neil and Brennan.

Throughout the campaign, there was opposition from Scalli supporters and others in town. Mayor Hynes's office put a lot of pressure on my supporters who worked for the city. Some of my friends who worked for the city even had Scalli stickers on their cars. However, they assured me that stickers don't vote, people do.

Another source of consternation came from young guys who hung out on the street corners. As I passed, they would needle me about having gone to Harvard. At first, it bothered me, until someone finally explained the reception I was getting on the street corners. He told me it is easy to criticize a Harvard guy and that's what they were doing. However, he said that despite their criticism, they would still support me because of my qualifications, including having gone to Harvard. Of course, they would never admit it. Election Day came, and despite a rocky start, I was re-elected and retained my seat in the legislature.

That year we had a newly elected governor, Foster Furcolo from Springfield. Our Speaker of the House, John Thompson of Ludlow, and Governor Furcolo collaborated to prorate a sales tax for Massachusetts. The House Chamber members were narrowly divided, with about five more Democratic members than Republican members. All my friends and advisors from Charlestown unanimously warned me that it would be politically fatal for me to support such a tax. Despite the cooperation of the speaker and governor, the sales tax bill came before the House for a vote. The bill failed to pass by three votes! One of those nay votes was mine.

The new Furcolo administration was incensed by the failure of the sales tax bill to pass. Those of us who voted against it were punished and denied any summer jobs for high school and college kids in our districts. No jobs for young people in Charlestown was tough to explain.

Representative Tom Doherty from Medford, who served in the legislature with me, was very wise about the workings of the House of Representatives. We became very friendly over our years serving in the House. Tom had voted for the sales tax. He was a recognized friend of the Furcolo administration. However, Tom was not unsympathetic to my being *persona non-grata* because of my vote against the sales tax. One day he came to me and asked me for a vote on a matter he was interested in. Since the bill had no effect on my district, I gave it to him. A couple of times over the next month or so, at his request, I gave him several votes on matters that had no effect on Charlestown. As we were going into an afternoon session, Tom told me how he appreciated my votes. Tom then said that he could help with getting some summer jobs for kids in my district under his name. He helped over one hundred kids from Charlestown get jobs that year.

The Furcolo Administration considered Tom Doherty as the helpful Doherty. By contrast, I was considered a rebel. Over time, my status as a rebel abated because I was a very active member of the House Education Committee. Governor Furcolo was committed to overhauling secondary education and favored a network of community colleges. I was very helpful to his effort. With some luck and persistence, I was ultimately able to sponsor a community college on the edge of Charlestown.

Charlestown boasted the oldest state prison in the Commonwealth. Built in 1805, the prison was a blight on the neighborhood. Over the years, pressure mounted in the community to get rid of the one hundred and fifty year old state prison. Near the end of my first term, there was a massive prison break. The State National Guard arrived with tanks and heavily armed soldiers. There was fear, anger, confusion and disbelief throughout the community. I joined a group of members of the Charlestown community to fight for abandonment of the prison.

As coincidence would have it, the community college initiative coincided with the mounting community pressure to get rid of the prison. The site was the perfect place for one of the new community colleges. The prison was torn down and one of Massachusetts' first community colleges rose in its place. Serendipitously, the EL was dismantled and the tracks relocated to a commercial area on the edge of the community to the new school area. A stop in front of the college was readily engineered and the whole area became a booming center!

As an aside, the transportation system enabled people to attend Bunker Hill Community College and commute on the public MBTA. These developments in a short five-year period caused Charlestown to boom, and helped to revive the community with a surge in the number of working professionals who moved into the area. Today, Bunker Hill Community College has an enrollment of sixteen thousand students.

Throughout my time in the legislature, I took my father's advice to put the people of Charlestown first. The Bunker Hill Monument, a 293-foot high obelisk dating back to the 1840s and commemorating the Battle of Bunker Hill, is one of the most important landmarks in Charlestown. About halfway through my second term, while wandering around Monument Square, I met the mother of one of my campaign workers. She was very outspoken. She angrily snapped, "Gerry, can't you do something about cleaning up our monument? It's neglected and dirty!" The next day, while attending the legislative session working on passing the budget, I talked to my old friend and mentor Cornelius Desmond. He listened and sat quietly for a few minutes; then he perked up with a smile. He had an idea for the budget. The House was controlled by Democrats – but barely. The Speaker needed votes for a bill. I could help him. With the Speaker and Desmond's help, we got an addition to the budget to preserve specific historic sites. Ultimately, the addition was approved by both the House of Representatives and later the Senate. Twenty-five thousand dollars was allotted to clean the Bunker Hill Monument. Thus, the historic obelisk was cleaned for the first time since it was completed in 1843. The people of Charlestown were pleased and grateful. However, one of my adversaries spread the word that, "the only thing Doherty has done for Charlestown is get the tall column cleaned. All we got was the shaft."

In 1959, there was a mayoral election to elect Mayor John Hynes's successor. It is an understatement to say there was a crowded field in the primary. Candidates included John E. Powers, President of the Massachusetts Senate, and John Collins, a former state senator and then current Registrar of Probate. Collins had lost to Mayor Hynes four years earlier in a close election. As an adult, Collins was confined to a wheelchair because he had been ill with polio. Other candidates running in the primary were John McMorrow, a former legislator and a current school committee member, and Senator James Hennigan of Jamaica Plain.

Hennigan was my friend so I decided to support him. At that time, I was going to law school and exams were imminent. I told Hennigan I would help but I would not be available until school finished, after the Bunker Hill Day Parade. The day before the parade, Marilyn called me at my office at the State House. She was in tears. She said there were two men at our door who wanted to come into the house with a cylinder of helium. She put them on the phone. They explained that they worked for Hennigan and they would like to use our basement to blow up balloons to distribute during the parade. After calming Marilyn down, I gave them permission to do so.

That night we had visitors, and my cousin from Brooklyn stayed overnight. Since we didn't have a guest room, my cousin stayed in our bedroom on the second floor and Marilyn and I slept on our pullout couch in the first-floor living room. As we put out the light and settled in, we both began to hear *pop, pop* followed by a whole symphony of bursts. We got up and rushed to the cellar door and opened it. At the bottom of the stairs, our two cats were batting and picking at the array of balloons. We went back to bed, serenaded by the sounds of exploding balloons all night.

After the Bunker Hill Day Parade, I began chaperoning Jim Hennigan's wife, Marjorie, to various shopping areas across the city. It was a simple task. I would go to a shopping center in one of the political wards, such as Brighton, approach shoppers to introduce myself, and then introduce Marjorie. "This is Marjorie Hennigan, whose husband, Senator Jim Hennigan, is running for Mayor of Boston." Reactions varied. Some just nodded, others would shake their head, some would briefly converse, and others would just brush past us. Marge was a very attractive woman with a pleasant personality. She weathered these meetings with strangers very well.

After about three weeks of doing this, I was walking around Charlestown on a Saturday morning. The father of one of my grammar school classmates passed by and we started to chat. As I told him what I was doing for Jim Hennigan, he interrupted me and said "Gerard, look around here. All you see are 'Powers' signs on the houses. No one knows your friend Hennessey or Harrington or whatever his name is. Powers is very strong in this town. When he wins, they will come after you and crush you. If I were you, I would get my ass back here and work for Charlestown. Just remember, stay close to the people in this town." Both embarrassed and a bit rattled, I thanked him and went away depressed. He was right. By working for Hennigan, I was taking the people of Charlestown for granted. When I asked several friends what they thought, they sheepishly said. "He is right!"

I explained to the Hennigans that I could only help on their campaign on a limited basis because I had to spend time in my own district. For the rest of July and August, Marilyn and I focused on my own politicking. Marilyn was great. Every other week she had a ladies' tea night at our home. At each one of the functions, we had about fifty or sixty guests. I would appear briefly, shake hands and say a few words about Charlestown and about Hennigan's race for mayor. The teas were very well received.

Unfortunately, Hennigan's mayoral campaign did not fare well. Collins and Powers won the primary. Hennigan did poorly across the city. He even lost his home district. Surprisingly, however, George Frazier, the well-read political columnist for the Boston Herald, wrote a commentary about the primary in which he noted "the emergence of Gerard Doherty of Charlestown as the new political ward boss!!" Frazier wrote, "With Doherty's backing in Charlestown, Hennigan lost by only forty-four votes. ... Doherty is one of our promising new leaders."

After Hennigan's loss, I stayed neutral. Collins ended up beating Powers in the final election. The people in the Collins administration who controlled his patronage jobs, housing and other municipal activities, made a determined effort to freeze me and my friends out of anything to do with the city. In the early summer of 1960, they achieved their goal of punishing me. For more than a hundred years, the Bunker Hill Day Parade route passed by my house on Washington Street. Because of pressure from some of my local enemies, the Collins administration moved the parade off Washington Street to the adjoining Rutherford Avenue, where very few people lived. The route change resulted in nasty criticism of Mayor Collins. In my neighborhood, even people who were not friendly with me were so insulted and infuriated that they became my supporters. The change in the parade route backfired. The following year, the parade returned to Washington Street, where it continues to this day. However, I became a thorn in Mayor Collins's side in the state legislature. I opposed everything he wanted and could convince many friends in the House from outside Boston to join me in opposing some of his bills.

Another memorable moment I experienced while serving in the House occurred when I introduced a bill to require a session of the House to open with a prayer, and, in particular, a Catholic prayer. When the bill came up for a vote, one of my best friends and a very good guy voted against the bill. I was dumfounded. I approached David to ask about his vote and he responded that he just didn't like the idea of mandating a prayer, and then with a wink he added, "besides, I am an Episcopalian." Again, I learned the lesson of not assuming anything about a person.

Building a Law Practice

In 1960, I had just graduated from Suffolk University Law School. Politically, I was not very active and I had no real opposition for my re-election to the legislature. After winning my primary election, I spent that fall preparing for the bar exam, which was held right after Christmas. I called it my scholastic hibernation. The only time I went out was the night before the final election for the Presidency, November 8, when John F. Kennedy had a mammoth rally at the Boston Garden. After the rally, which was a tremendous success, I squirreled back to my studies for the remaining months.

Kennedy was elected President after a long night. One of the great articles recounting John Kennedy's election was a story attributed to Dave Powers, a Charlestown native who was one of John Kennedy's oldest and most trusted aides. Supposedly in discussion with the newly-elected President, a reporter credited his success to three great schools, "Harvard, Yale and Princeton." Dave Powers then interrupted the reporter, "You were right about three schools but those schools were St. Mary's, St. Francis's and St. Catherine's." All schools in Charlestown.

The bar exam was a two-day ordeal between Christmas and New Year's Day. Early in January, I was inducted to the legislature for my third term. It was a hectic three month waiting for the bar exam results. There were a lot of prayers and worried expectations. In mid-April, I was notified that I had passed the bar. My legislative colleagues, Senator Jim Hennigan and Representative William Bulger from South Boston, later President of the Massachusetts State Senate, invited me to join their law firm at 11 Beacon Street. My law practice centered pretty much on appearances for defendants charged with petty crimes before the Charlestown District Court. I was always busy, but most of my clients were non-paying and mostly juveniles. Eventually, I decided to stop handling criminal cases.

In the early sixties, I became acquainted with Ed Fish, owner of Peabody Construction Company. He had a couple of problems with a partner, which I was able to resolve. He later asked me to act as his lawyer. He and I worked together on a real estate project in Lowell. I was his lawyer. It was a one hundred unit, low-income housing complex sponsored by the Lowell Junior Chamber of Commerce. Everything worked out well and from that time on a wonderful partnership developed between us. Over the years, the two of us were involved with about fifty various housing developments. We never had any fights or disagreements, nor did we have any written agreements. Our word was enough. Our relationship lasted for more than thirty-five years, ending with his sudden death in 2010.

Probably one of our most interesting housing developments was the development of ninety units of affordable housing in the abandoned Vermont State Prison in the late 1970s. Interestingly, our involvement with the prison started with a high school student intern. In the spring of 1975, my associate Kevin Leary, a Georgetown College graduate, interviewed prospective candidates for Georgetown University. In March, he interviewed a young man, Paul Dello Iacono, who was graduating the following June. Kevin was impressed by Paul, whose father was handicapped, and who was trying to get a scholarship to attend college. After Kevin Leary's meeting with him, Kevin was very moved by the boy's story. However, Kevin thought that his chances of acceptance at Georgetown were not very good. We liked him so we decided that he could work in our law office as an intern on Thursdays, the only day he was available. Paul was very resourceful. He could do almost anything. He could fix and manage some of our old broken down duplicating machines and recording equipment. After Paul was accepted at St. Anselm College in New Hampshire, we offered him a job for the summer. He was a very energetic and a diligent worker.

Our office had subscribed to the New England Real Estate Journal, which arrived twice a month. Paul read it closely. Early in August, when the Journal arrived, there was a story about the state of Vermont auctioning off their recently closed state prison in Windsor. Paul thought that we might be interested in it. I quickly dismissed the whole idea as being crazy. Two weeks later, the next edition of the Journal arrived. When I came into the office very early one morning, Paul was looking at one of the articles in the new Journal. He said to me very seriously, "You really ought to think about buying this prison." I felt guilty that several weeks earlier I had summarily dismissed Paul's suggestion about the prison as naïve. I asked him what he knew about the sale. He showed me the advertisement in the latest Journal. It stated that the prison was being auctioned off that day and bids would be accepted up to 3 o'clock that afternoon. The more I listened to him the more I began to think about it.

Coincidentally, my good friend and partner, Ed Fish, called me to discuss jobs we were working on. At an attempt at levity, I said, "How would you like to buy a prison?" Ed responded quickly, "I've tried my whole life to stay out of prison and now you want me to buy one!" He asked me what I knew about the sale of the prison. I told him I was holding the folder in front of me. He said, "Maybe I might be interested in it for short money." Thus, we both agreed to put up ten thousand dollars each and make a bid of twenty thousand dollars for the purchase of the Vermont State prison. After some more musing and discussion, we became very serious and decided we would make a serious and competitive bid. So ultimately, we decided on a bid of twenty-seven thousand, five hundred dollars.

Our bid had to be accompanied by a certified check of 5 percent for our proposal. Paul stated that a plane was leaving for Vermont in about two hours. Arrangements were made for Paul to get on the plane with the appropriate certified check to the state purchasing agent to validate our proposal. My day became very busy with other business activities that required my involvement. At about five o'clock, my assistant came in and said there was a man on the phone from Vermont. I picked up the phone. It was the state purchasing agent, who asked me to identify myself, which I did. He then said, "I'm holding a valid check for 5 percent of the purchase price of our state prison and the check is from you, is that so?" I agreed, and he said, "Today you have bought the Vermont State Prison and we will send all of the information to you when we have it available."

The following weekend my wife and I were at our country house in western Massachusetts. I suggested that we take an hour-and-a-half trip to look at our newly purchased prison. She readily agreed. We drove by the prison and viewed it from the outside. Marilyn noted that a few blocks from the prison there was the office of the local newspaper. She could see some activity in its large picture window. "Maybe it's time for you to go in and identify yourself and preclude all sorts of wild rumors on what you are going to do with the prison," Marilyn said. I followed her advice. I went in and chatted with the editor; he seemed pleased to get the information. The following week he wrote a brief but clear story as to who we were and what we were going to do.

Two weeks later the board of selectmen of Winsor had a meeting to work out the details of our purchase. Three of us went to the session late one afternoon. We all met outside the town hall. We were all dressed very conservatively in white shirts, simple ties and blue suits. We went into the meeting, which started immediately. All five selectmen sat at a table. They were all dressed in lumberjack shirts. Just as the chairman gaveled the meeting to order, one of the selectman asked us if we were representing some kind of a religious group and if we were planning on incorporating some kind of a mental facility at the prison. We explained that we were developers and we wanted to convert the prison into about eighty units of affordable housing for middle-income people. There was some discussion, but it was all very favorable to our proposal. The board voted to affirm our group as the legal owner of the property.

Over the next few months we had several other positive meetings with town hall and the board of selectmen. We went through the normal process of hearings and meetings. Our architect, Timothy Anderson of Boston, a graduate of Harvard and Harvard Architectural School, was at our first session. We also presented the credentials of the construction company, which was owned by Ed Fish. I gave detailed background of my legal experience. Our construction started quite soon after the permitting and the conversion of the various buildings, which made up the prison complex. It took about eight to nine months to complete our undertaking. We scheduled a public showing in late August, which lasted for two days. We had over one thousand people from the town and surrounding areas view the completed facility. All the elected officials from the State of Vermont were there, and all who visited our site seemed to be happy and enthused.

Still working in the legislature, by my third term in the House, I had fully developed my profile. Some thought I had big elbows and others were just plain critical. One legislator described me as looking like a taxi cab with its back doors open – in reference to my big ears. Another comment was that my personal appearance resembled an unmade bed. One reporter considered me stiff and arrogant. He referred to me as wearing three-piece pajamas. Notwithstanding these descriptions, I just padded along. My major effort now was to focus on getting an ice skating rink in Charlestown. Persistence and friendship paid off. I got the project funded. Two of my final necessary votes I got from Republicans from Pittsfield. Everyone was ecstatic. The Metropolitan District Commission was given the responsibility to prepare and build the rink. Things went along well.

Since land mass for it was scarce, the decision was to build it on the abandoned Emmons Playground, which was a rusty eyesore. Everyone was pleased. However, when the final plans were finished by the state planners, there was a need to acquire the area at the far end of the project. It was suggested that three homes would have to be taken by eminent domain. One of them was the Horrigan family home. Their son, John "Hock" Horrigan, was a very close friend and teammate of mine on the "Washies." In the cellar of his home, our football team had a much-enjoyed meeting place. Hock, a seventeen-year-old sailor was killed on the cruiser Indianapolis in the South Pacific on the last day of World War II.

Robert Murphy, former Lieutenant Governor, was head of the group in charge of building the rink. I visited them together with my local pals who knew Hock; we pleaded with the building committee to redesign and alter the project so that it could fit on a site that would save the Horrigan's home. Efforts were made to redesign and reshape the rink, but to no avail. Murphy was cooperative but no feasible solution was possible. Some of his assistants worried that if the allocated money was not used in a reasonable time, the money would be taken for another project. I was told by my legislature leaders to use the appropriation quickly and perhaps, later, another site in Charlestown would be found.

After a long discussion with a half dozen of my closest friends and advisors, we had to go forward with the building of the rink over the designated area. The Horrigans and two other families lost their homes. The Horrigans moved. I lost the friendship of a wonderful family. They lost their son to the war and their home to my plan. It was one of the most difficult things I had to do. It is still a haunting memory of a broken friendship.

I was no longer in the legislature when the rink was finished in 1965, but my successor, Tony Scalli, called me. Both of us got along well. The dedication of the rink was scheduled some time in the early spring. It was to be named after Frederick D. Emmons, for whom the area was originally named. I had suggested to Tony that John Horrigan's name be added to the name of the rink, and everyone agreed. Today the name of the rink is Emmons Horrigan O'Neill Memorial Rink. Still guilt ridden, I thought it would be an insult to the Horrigan family if I attended the dedication. About a week before the event, Tony Scalli, who was to preside over the affair, called me and asked me to be the major speaker at the ceremony. I thanked him but said I did not think it appropriate, or to the liking of the Horrigan family. He said "Gerry, they are the ones that asked you to be the speaker and said that you were Johnny's friend." The day was unforgettable; John's three sisters and brother shook my hand and thanked me for my comments and all my efforts.

In 1961, my friend Bob Quinn finally brought Mayor Collins and me together. We shook hands and had a friendly chat. Shortly after our meeting, I was able to help him on some matters. Unexpectedly, he sent for me and thanked me for my new-found support. Then he surprised me. He said he would make available five hundred thousand dollars for improvements in Charlestown. I was stunned. That evening when I got home, my father was visiting. I talked to him about Charlestown's good fortune and asked what I should do. I then relayed a story to my father. Late in February, I had received a call from a Charlestown woman who complained that the gas street light outside her home had blown out. Her call was one of many I received about other street lights blowing out. Most of the calls were from women who were afraid to walk the street in the darkness. My father had better street sense than I. He said instantly, "What about using that money Collins is making available? It's a win-win for him as mayor and you as the resourceful and effective representative." I responded, "I will ask Collins to designate the money for the street light program." My father then got very serious and said, "Get after that project, but don't do your street until last just in case the money runs out." The light project was a huge success, praised by almost everyone. As my father predicted, the city ran out of money to replace the gas lights in my home precinct. Ironically, today this area of Charlestown is considered quaint and mellow because of the gas lights, and is known as the "Gas Light District."

While I was in the State House, Frank Morrissey, John F. Kennedy's local secretary, was very good to me. He had been a longtime friend of the Kennedys, especially their father, Joseph Kennedy, Sr. Frank was also a native of Charlestown and the oldest of six children. When he was younger he used to get up at four o'clock in the morning to sell newspapers outside the Navy Yard. The Charlestown Navy Yard was the oldest ship-building facility in the country. It ceased operations in 1974 but remains home to the U.S.S. Constitution. In the 1940s, some eight thousand men and women were employed there. As Morrissey got older, he became very active in the Charlestown community.

When I was elected to the House of Representatives, Frank was very supportive of me and the needs of my district. At Christmastime, the post offices would hire a lot of temporary help to handle the heavy load of holiday mail and gifts. Finding employment for my constituents was a big concern. Frank was able to get many of them temporary jobs at the post office. Sometimes he assisted me with nearly one hundred applicants a year.

Also at Christmastime, the Navy Yard had a half dozen specialty shops – electrical, welding, blacksmith, maintenance groups – that would each have individual holiday parties for Charlestown kids. The shops would always have an oversupply of gifts. Frank arranged for me to get the surplus, which I would distribute to families in need throughout Charlestown. For years, many people in town called me the "bag man."

Meeting Edward M. Kennedy

In 1961, Frank Morrissey called to tell me that the President's youngest brother, Ted, was thinking of running for the United States Senate. There was to be a special election to fill the seat formerly occupied by the President. Rumor had it that Edward J. McCormack, Jr., the Attorney General, was going to run. Morrissey wanted me to arrange for a meeting of ten or so state legislators to vet the idea of Ted running before it became public. We were to meet for lunch at Locke-Ober's, an exclusive Boston restaurant. At first, Representative William Bulger was reluctant to go. However, he was encouraged to do so by Governor's Councilor Sonny McDonough, not a fan of the Kennedys, who told Bulger he should order the most expensive thing on the menu. Bulger and other legislators came to the lunch. As directed, Bulger ordered the most expensive item on the menu, Lobster Savannah. Teddy was paying for it with money he borrowed from his sister Eunice. As I tried to have Bulger speak up for Kennedy as the others had, Kennedy was staring at the bill. He then joked, "We have to stop talking to Bulger…. we can't afford him. He ordered the Lobster Savannah, which is twenty-four dollars." We all laughed. It was a good first meeting. On the way out of the luncheon, we ran into Bill Lewis, a political reporter for the Boston Globe. He knew something was up. I brushed him off and just said, "Hello."

A week after that luncheon, Frank Morrissey called me again to ask if I could arrange another lunch with ten different members of the legislature. This second lunch was also held at Locke-Ober's. Again, as we were leaving, I ran into Bill Lewis. He saw all the legislators and wanted to know what was going on. I did not give him any kind of an answer and kept on moving. The following Sunday Lewis wrote a featured article in the Globe about the meetings I was having at Locke-Ober's with the legislators and Ted Kennedy. He mentioned how I was exposing myself to the anger of the many longshoremen and freight handlers who had already voiced their support for Ed McCormack as the Democratic candidate in the primary election for senator.

That Sunday I was out all day and had not gotten a chance to read the article. I went to Mass in the morning and then saw a football game in the afternoon. When I got home, my wife said to me, "There is some nut who has been calling all day trying to imitate a Kennedy. I'm busy and I don't appreciate the joke." At which point the phone rang again and the caller said he was looking for "Gerald." Marilyn handed me the phone. It was Ted Kennedy. He apologized for putting me on the spot in the newspaper and he was upset that I might be in a lot of trouble with people in Charlestown. I said, somewhat gallantly, "Don't worry about me, I can take care of myself." He asked me if I could come to his house at 3 Charles River Square and visit with him, which I did. I liked him and I told him I would support him regardless of the consequences to me.

Around this time, when I was working with Ted Kennedy, I became friendly with Bill McCarthy, head of the local Teamsters group, which had its headquarters in Charlestown and the National Teamsters Union. He was a cousin of my late friend Margaret Crotty's mother. She introduced me to McCarthy, letting him know how close I was to her. Those days were very troubling and confusing for the Teamsters. Attorney General Robert Kennedy was pursuing Jimmy Hoffa, head of the National Teamsters Union. Hoffa had suddenly disappeared. There was bad blood between the Teamsters and the Kennedys, but I was able to smooth things out and bring together Ted Kennedy and Bill McCarthy. At first, there was marked stress in the relationship, but gradually it softened and the two became politely cordial, working together to solve Massachusetts' labor problems.

After I became friendly with Bill McCarthy, he introduced me to the local president of the Longshoreman's Association 799, which had a large membership from Charlestown. Together with some other local leaders, a local community action agency, named the Kennedy Center, was founded in Charlestown. It was funded by local leaders, Bill McCarthy of the Teamsters, and me. It became a very helpful and effective action center, offering social and community health services. However, its most active and successful undertaking was its counseling services for local high school students, providing tutorial and employment services that assisted countless youth in gaining college educations.

This very popular and local organization operated for many years and achieved great success with Charlestown. Today, a scaled down version of the Kennedy Center is still active in Charlestown. It is primarily involved with social welfare programs.

Early in 1962, my duties as Vice Chairman of the Committee on Education required my presence at a lot of testimonials. Usually, I rented a tuxedo. Finally, my assistant Elinore bought me a tuxedo from Filene's Basement for an event I was scheduled to go to with Ted Kennedy. After everyone had left my office at 11 Beacon Street, I put on my new tuxedo. I tried to pull up my pants zipper but it was stuck and would not work. I imagined I would have to hold the program brochure in front of my zipper all night. Thankfully, early in my years in the legislature I became very friendly with a Chinese tailor, Harry Chin, who was around the corner from the State House. I brought all my cleaning and clothing repairs to him. I walked from my office to Ted's house at Three Charles River Square, but on the way, I passed my close friend Harry Chin's shop. His light was still on and I rapped on his door. He quickly came to the door. I told him about my problem. He said, "No problem." He measured the opening. He then went to a rack of women skirts. He checked several of them and found an appropriate zipper. It was gold. He cut it out of the skirt and sewed it onto my pants. I happily went down to meet Ted with my new gold-zippered pants. I told Ted about my episode. He smiled and said, "Gerry, I always knew that you were golden!" For several years, I wore that tuxedo without a problem.

About a year later, I had another problem that I thought Harry Chin could solve. I had a wonderful light blue suit that I wore consistently in the summer months. However, the knees of the pant leg started to show stains from so much wear. I talked to Harry about what he could do. He said he would dye my favorite suit navy blue. About a week later my dyed suit was ready. I walked to his shop and put it on. It was very dark navy and looked great. I had a busy day scheduled at the State House. There were a couple of quick meetings I had to attend, and then I went to the patronage office to plead my case for more summer jobs for Charlestown kids. I started to talk with a woman about jobs; then, in the middle of the discussion, she halted me and said, "You have spilled grape juice or something on your shirt." She said, "Stand up." I did. There was a blue stain blossoming all over the front of my shirt. She said, "Take off your jacket. Your back is all blue, too." I went to the nearest men's room and took off my jacket and tee shirt. My body was blue. I went directly to Filene's Basement and bought myself a new dark grey suit. When I got home, I showered for a half-an-hour to erase the blue coloring from my body. After that, I went back to the State House and continued my normal activities. It took me almost a week to fully get the blue dye off my body.

Campaigning with Ted Kennedy

During the Christmas holidays, Ted Kennedy usually went away skiing. The winter months were very slow with a limited number of activities. Town committees would have meetings, and we would try to attend as many of them as we could. Generally, I would go campaigning with Ted once or twice a week. To prepare for these meetings, I would talk to legislators from that town. Then, I would write up background notes to give to Ted beforehand. These notes would include the names and information concerning important people he would meet. Increasingly, he relied upon these notes and my going to the meetings with him. For example, if he were going to Somerville, I would talk to legislators about who was and who was not important in Somerville, as well as issues of local concern. In New Bedford, I was very friendly with one of the representatives, Tony Silva. Silva would give me a good outline as to who was important and who was not important for Ted Kennedy to talk with.

As we began to move around the state, people began to take us more seriously. Initially, some thought that Ted Kennedy assumed he could just clap his hands and expect everyone to fall in line for him. There was a lot of resentment towards him trying to start at the top. We began to face more opposition with a great deal of criticism coming from the more politically active people who had some connection to Ed McCormack, the Attorney General. McCormack treated people very well. In return, he received a great deal of support. Furthermore, he provided an incentive to his associates who would back him. Namely, he would appoint lawyers as Assistant Attorney General. None of them worked as an Assistant Attorney General, nor were they were paid as such. It was merely a clever technique, appointing them for the sake of the title, which would benefit the person's law businesses. These lawyers with this title generally lived in small communities like New Bedford. The title of Assistant Attorney General enhanced their professional reputations. It was a huge benefit to McCormack who could highlight the fact that he had local relationships and he wasn't just coming in from Washington expecting people to vote for him. Ted's campaign was difficult at times. Some of McCormack's supporters became very negative. We began to see all sorts of critical commentaries about Ted in letters to the editors.

Many local radio stations also started to really bang away at Ted. It was always the same thing, "Here's a guy who has never worked a day in his life, and he wants to start at the top." They were very difficult to deal with. We just kept struggling along. We would be going off to some ward committee meeting and because Teddy did more and more of them, I would write a little background report for him, but I wouldn't go with him. However, over a period of time, Teddy began to feel that I had a better sense of political repertoire than he, and so I would go and visit with some of the people who were attending his functions. Because of the radio stations banging away at Ted, we had problems with some people in these communities who thought Ted Kennedy couldn't put a coherent sentence together.

All along the stump, he had a lot to learn and we had a lot to learn from Teddy.

We continued to attend town committees. At one of those meetings in Somerville, I ran into an old friend of mine; a fellow by the name of Bill Joyce. He and I played football together at Malden Catholic. Bill walked right up to Ted and said, "I'm with you, Ted." Teddy sort of swelled his chest a little bit and gloated. Joyce then said, "The reason I'm with you is this. You see that guy over there with the glasses, Doherty? If I wasn't with you, he would beat the hell out of me. He was the meanest, roughest football player I ever played with. But ya know, he kept me in line. That is why I am with you tonight! In my ward, you'll get all the votes!"

April was kind of slow and draggy. Ted and I continued to go out a couple times a week to some ward or city committee meetings. It was sort of drudgery by then. So, one day I came up with the thought, "Why don't I find out how we are doing across the state?" We had seen enough city and ward committees; we had plenty of stories in the newspaper. I decided to try to conduct some sort of informal, intelligent survey among the members of the legislature. The first district that would be reporting at the state convention was the First Berkshire District. So, I went out to the First Berkshire District, where most of the delegates came out of Pittsfield, followed by North Adams.

This is how it worked. For example, in North Adams, they had five wards, and each ward had one delegate to the convention. Furthermore, if, in a ward, Ted Kennedy received more than one thousand votes, he would gain an extra delegate. If he received two thousand votes in that ward, he would gain another extra delegate. In Pittsfield, the same organizational plan figured into our calculations. As I best remember, there were seven or eight wards in Pittsfield. I tried to figure out how well we were going to do. I spent a majority of an afternoon talking to the representative from North Adams. He gave me a very candid appraisal of how we were doing. Then I would do the same with the representative from Pittsfield. Over a week and a half, I interviewed members from all the cities and towns.

Boston had twenty-two wards. Because Boston was a city, it got one delegate and each of its twenty-two wards would also get a delegate. Boston was a gold mine of delegates, as were most cities. Worcester ranked second and Springfield third, followed by the cities of New Bedford, Fall River and Cambridge. The rest of the cities were relatively small. Some towns, like Belmont, had a very large population, but because they weren't a city, the distribution of the delegates was different.

Meeting President Kennedy in the Oval Office

By the late spring of 1962, I had completed the compilation of where Ted's strengths were, based on information I was able to gather from individual members of the legislature. I finished the brief and handed it to Ted, who was impressed.

It was close to Easter. Ted got a call from President Kennedy to go down to Palm Beach for Easter. Ted left on a Friday. On Saturday, the President talked with him. "My sources in Massachusetts indicate that you are not doing very well. Our contacts think you are going to have a problem. What do you know about this? Tell me something that they don't know." A lot of the President's advisors didn't want Ted to run because they thought that if he lost it would reflect poorly on the President. They were afraid he would lose and people would start to get tired of too many Kennedys. They were not very sympathetic. Teddy said, "Well…yes! I have a summary of my campaign status." The President said, "Well this afternoon will be rather slow, why don't we sit down and look at the summary."

When they met later, Ted produced the book I had put together and handed it to the President. About halfway through, the President said, "Where did you get all this? Whoever put it together knows what he is talking about – and who is that?" Ted said, "Gerry Doherty." The President said, "Oh, I know him." The President was pleased, but was still very troubled about the campaign. "We have to stay very close to this, Teddy. The next week or so is going to determine if you're going to run."

Ted returned from Palm Beach on the following Monday. When I walked over to the Bowdoin Street office, the people in Ted's office said they had been looking for me all day. I was then informed that I had been scheduled to go to Washington the following Friday with Maurice Donahue, who was a Kennedy supporter and president in the Massachusetts Senate. Maurice knew the President well. Our trip seemed like a big secret. I had no idea why I was being summoned to Washington and neither did Maurice. Even our plane tickets were under different names.

When we got to the White House, Maurice and I were ushered into the Oval Office. Shortly after, people we knew from Massachusetts who were working in the White House came in and all settled around the oval table. The President walked in and sat right across from us. In front of him was the book that I had compiled for Teddy. The President stood up and said, "All of you people are from Massachusetts and it's very important to me that my brother do well. We're going to do everything we can to help! That's why Gerry and Maurice are here today."

We all sat down and the President started to flip through the book. Maurice, who was the senior member of the Massachusetts delegation, sat directly in front of the President. I sat a couple of chairs away from Maurice. Starting with the First Senatorial District, the Berkshires, the President knew some of the people and would say a few words about each of them. As he went on to the next district, the President started asking Maurice specific questions about the delegates. Maurice kept turning to me to get the answers. Noticing this, the President asked me to change seats with Maurice so he could ask me questions directly. Hopefully, I would have the answers. It was amazing how much he knew about many of the individuals who were listed in the book as delegates.

We got through about ten districts when there was a tremendous noise on the White House lawn as a helicopter descended. The President said, "Oh, I have to leave. That's Prime Minister Harold Macmillan. Can you fellows stay over and talk with Bobby?" We agreed. He also added that his political reputation was on the line and everyone was expected to work hard on Ted's election. Not all of the President's aides were in favor of Ted's run for the Senate seat, nor of me being the campaign manager.

The next day, at about eleven o'clock, we went to the Attorney General's office. Bobby Kennedy came in with his secretary, Angie Novello, who sat in and took notes. Bobby went through the book and was tough on the questioning. "How do you know that so and so is very favorable and can be helpful?" and "How do you know this guy?" For the most part, I had the right answers, or at least believable answers. I responded with a little story about each legislator and how I got to know him, or how he was friendly with another legislator. After about an hour of this, we had gone through maybe five more districts and he said, "Okay Gerry, you're going to be in charge!" "In charge of what?" I stuttered. He said, "You are going to be in charge of the Ted's convention campaign. You're going to help us." This set me back. He said, "You are going to be in control and you're going to make the major calls." Bobby then said, "We'll have some people up there Monday to give you a hand. Anyone that gives you a hard time, you can call Angie here and we will get after them, or you can call me. Here are my numbers. My home number, my personal number, and here is Angie's number. Thank you!" With that, Bobby left.

On the plane ride back to Boston, Maurice laughed and said, "I don't know what the hell all that means, Gerry. You seem to talk in parables, but do you know what you just got us into?"

Monday, I went back to my regular routine, wandered through Charlestown then went to my office. When I got to the State House, Bartley Joyce, one of the pages said to me, "People across the street, at the Bowdoin Street headquarters, have been looking for you all morning!" I sauntered over to the headquarters. The office was all excited and they told me I needed to be there later that afternoon because a special team was coming up from Washington to see me. This team was going to set up a voter retrieval system to determine where our votes were coming from. They said "You need to be here at four o'clock." I said, "Do you want Maurice?" They said, "No. That's not necessary."

I headed over at four o'clock. When I got there, I noticed three people who had all worked on the President's campaign in West Virginia and some of the harder states. One of them was Dave Hackett, a classmate of Bobby Kennedy's at Milton

Academy. He was a great hockey player, and a great systems person. When John F. Kennedy ran for President, he set up a retrieval system of votes for the tough states and it worked out well. He explained to us what we had to do and how we needed to set up a control room. The control room would be manned by four women. We would break the state up into forty senatorial districts. Each woman would be assigned ten districts. They would then compile all the information they could about delegates and local issues, tracking newspapers and any significant occurrences in their respective districts. Each would track all the delegates, all the newspapers, and all significant occurrences in their respective districts. Every afternoon at four o'clock I would quiz the women on each of their districts. Each woman became an expert on their respective districts' activities. For example, the woman who had the First Berkshire District knew at least how we thought respective delegates were going to vote. She had the list of all the delegates, what they did and who they worked for. We referred to this information gathering office as the "boiler room."

The woman handling the Berkshires read the Berkshire Eagle and could tell you who died in Berkshire County and who didn't die in Berkshire County. That same format applied to all the other ladies. It was my responsibility from about four to six o'clock each day to find out what they knew, what was happening in each district, and how certain situations should be handled. It was my job to find a remedy for each problem. That was our schedule for about two-and-a-half weeks. We dictated Ted's activities, including where he was going and what places we needed him to visit.

The State Democratic Convention

In June, we moved our group up to Springfield late on a Monday. The convention for senator was going to be on Friday. We were set up in huge hotel suites. One of the things that amazed me was the fact that Ted's team brought in their own switchboard! They did this because four years earlier, when there was an effort to nominate John F. Kennedy for Vice President, they ran into difficulties trying to communicate with people because they were using regular phones. This time we wanted to be in control of our own communications via phones and messages.

Monday, we set up everything. Tuesday, Wednesday and Thursday, we started to review everything we had and what was missing. On Thursday, from mid-morning to mid-afternoon, a lot of local and national reporters from the New York Times, Herald Tribune, Boston Globe and local newspapers had been interviewing Steve Smith, who was Ted's brother-in-law and spokesperson.

At about four o'clock, Steve Smith said to me, "You are going to tell me how many votes we are going to get." and I said, "I think we're going to do okay." He said, "Okay is not okay. I want to see how good you are." I said, "Well, I don't know how good I am." Steve Smith said, "Well, I'll know how good you are and how accurate you are. You see, what I want you to do is give me a summary of how many votes were going to get." I said, "I don't know!" He said, "If you're as good as people say you are and as good as you think you are, you'll get it done." Determined to prove myself, I disappeared for about two hours. I scurried off to the control room and talked to the women. I went from woman to woman, district to district, and looked closely and hard at what our vote totals would be in each district. We did that then I asked them for a number. I was very insistent that they be very conservative, which they were. Then I met with Steve and he said, "Do you have that number?" I answered, "Oh well, shucks, I do, but….." "I don't want to hear any buts," he said. He told me to write the number on a white note card and place it in an envelope. He said, "We're going to seal it and I'm going to put it in my pocket." I said, "Then what do you do?" He said, "Then we'll see after the election on Friday night how either lucky or good you are."

The next day, before the convention got underway I had an unexpected encounter with Massachusetts Speaker John "Iron Duke" Thompson while I was on the podium checking the microphone prior to the start of convention business, a good practice during a hotly contested race.

The Speaker described himself as a "delightful rogue" but he had another side too. He was often a bully. As I was checking the microphone, the Speaker approached, followed by his ever-present entourage. He started to bump me away, using his six-foot-two, 225-pound frame. Much to his surprise, I bumped back and told him I was not intimidated and if he doubted my abilities he should check the newspaper report of a decade-old football game between Malden Catholic and Springfield Cathedral. He would see my name prominently mentioned. He backed off as bullies often do when challenged. One never knew when encountering the Speaker whether one would be greeted with a kiss or kick. Several months later, as we encountered one another in the State House, he said to me, "I read the write-up of that game you referenced during our encounter on the podium. You were not kidding, you were quite the player." I didn't have any more problems with the Speaker.

93

I soon learned that the Speaker had more to worry about than me. The President informed his brother Ted that the F.B.I. was about to indict the Speaker. Ted warned me and others to stay away from him. I organized a rebel group of legislators to start planning for a new day in the legislature. We held meetings outside the State House at a restaurant at the bottom of Beacon Hill. At one of these meetings, a young representative from Watertown, Paul Menton, at my urging made a proposal that I endorsed. Another member of the group stood up and declared it was a dumb suggestion. I reiterated my support for Paul and the objector countered with, "I could never understand how you got into Harvard and I didn't." I responded, "I got into Harvard because I got high marks on the morning aptitude test and on the afternoon achievement tests in Latin and Physics." My colleagues roared their approval.

Dirty tricks are always an issue in a campaign, so it is important that one be aware at all times. One night during the campaign, a call went out for volunteers to do a mailing. As I watched the volunteers come into the headquarters, I spied the girlfriend of one of my fellow representatives who was an ardent support of Eddie McCormack. She was politely asked to leave. Discovering the plant brought accolades from the other campaign professionals who now thought I was a really smart guy.

The next day was the convention. It wasn't even close. They stopped the roll call about halfway through and Ted was substantially ahead. Ted Kennedy won by acclamation and we were all excited. After it was over, Steve Smith motioned to me. He said, "Now we are going to see how good you are." He proceeded to open the envelope and take the card out. He laughed and said to me, "You're good! You were off by two votes." He smiled and slapped me on the back. Then, the next day, they voted on the Governor's party endorsement and I went off to Marilyn's cousin's in Pittsfield for the weekend. On Monday, I had the house to myself and the phone rang. It was Robert Kennedy. He said, "I had difficulty finding you, but I wanted you to know how grateful our family is. I wanted you to do something and you did it, and we will be forever grateful. Thank you very much."

The week after the convention, we spent a lot of time on the phone thanking people and writing notes to individuals who were particularly helpful at the convention, delivering their delegations, certain key legislators and others who were on Ted Kennedy's call list. Ted made the calls. I must say he was very diligent and very persistent about making the contacts. The following Saturday, Ted invited Marilyn and me to go down to the Cape to have dinner with him. We arrived about eleven o'clock. We had a light lunch and then the plan was to go water skiing. I had never water skied before, nor did I have a bathing suit. Ted found a bathing suit for me and off we went. Much to my amazement, I was able to get up on the skis. I started off good. However, my borrowed bathing suit was not doing so well and after five minutes it started to slide down. I had to either surrender to modesty or really make a scene. So, I tried to hold the bathing suit up and that was it. Everything went helter-skelter. Everyone laughed. Later that afternoon, we had a cookout with a fair number of Teddy's nonpolitical friends from his Harvard days and it was an enjoyable time.

Moving forward, we had to figure out where we were weak and where we were strong. Halfway through that week, Steve Smith said that he and I and John Dowd, who ran the advertising campaign for John F. Kennedy when he was elected, were going to meet. He said, "Both of you are good halves, but are not good wholes. We will get you two together to make a whole." So, I met John Dowd. He was a very prestigious looking man. He looked like Brian Ahearn, the movie star. He told me how nervous he was on election night, when Kennedy was not winning. At that time, he was owed three hundred thousand dollars in advertising fees and sometimes it's difficult getting money from losers. He thanked God JFK ended up winning.

In the beginning of the campaign, Ted was a raw candidate and sometimes not a very savvy candidate. I matched him in inexperience for running a Senate campaign, but I did have street smarts and knew how to change lemons into lemonade. These skills came into play when I arranged for a reception for Boston delegates to the upcoming Massachusetts convention at the Parker House in Boston, where Ted could introduce himself to the Boston delegates. Unbeknownst to me, there was a rumor sweeping the Boston political circles that the President and Speaker John McCormack, Edward McCormack's uncle, would sit down and settle on one candidate; so members of the delegation did not want to declare themselves for fear they would back the wrong horse. This was the reason no one showed for the reception. When I arrived, the room was empty. Fearing a catastrophe, I called my good friend Kevin Kelly in Charlestown and asked him to round up as many friends as he could, including their wives or girlfriends, and to come to the Parker House for a free party.

At seven that evening I spotted Ted getting out of a cab. He had no money, so I paid the cab. This had become a common occurrence, so I always carried some extra cash when I knew I would be with Ted.

I asked Ted why he was early and he responded it was because the reception was scheduled to begin at 7 p.m. When I said, "no, it is scheduled for 8 p.m.," he left to go to his apartment nearby on Bowdoin Street to do some work. I advised him to return at 8:15 p.m. and when he did, there was a full room. Ted spoke a few words, shook a few hands, and left smiling.

John Dowd was a good friend of Teddy's father. He also had a son, Roger, who had done some political work for me on other campaigns. Our role was to be combatants for Ted Kennedy. We had to develop some news releases and other things, but our major role, as time went by, was to become Teddy's representatives in dealing with our opponent, Edward McCormack.

We would meet on Thursdays in the "boiler room" with the four women who knew their districts so well. Every day, for ten minutes, I would go into their information center and ask questions. We would find out what the local newspapers were writing about. It was a very good way to stay in the know. These women were very effective at keeping in touch with their districts and throughout the summer we made visitations based on their findings.

Ted and I had a few interesting experiences on our town visitations. From the onset of Ted's campaign, we always followed the same regimen that his older brother, the President, laid out for him and used in his own campaign. The President was Ted's mentor during the campaign and he turned to him often for advice. Early in his first campaign, the President counseled him about how to schedule his day. "Start at 6:30 a.m. and visit the plants and factories where the workers are just going to work. Shake hands and say 'Hello.' After nine o'clock, drop by restaurants and clubs where people are still hanging around after breakfast. Middle morning, visit town halls, fire stations and city halls. Then drop into lunches like Kiwanis and Garden Clubs." (It was important for someone like me to go in and ask if it was appropriate for Ted to campaign there. Occasionally we would be waved off.) "Now most important, take time off from two o'clock to four o'clock." Emphatically, the President said, "Relax and get in the tub for about a half hour." The President was Ted's mentor throughout the campaign and he turned to him often for advice.

So, we followed the President's advice and stuck to that schedule. One time, Ted and I got up early in the morning and went to the plant gate at the Charlestown Navy Yard where two thousand people were working. We stood outside and greeted people as they came into work. It was pretty ho-hum, and then a fellow came along with a frown on his face and said, "Good luck!" with some degree of trepidation. Ted said, "Good morning, sir!" The man sort of scowled and said, "Hey kid, they keep saying you haven't worked a day in your life. Let me tell ya something, you haven't missed a Goddamn thing!" Everyone laughed.

Occasionally, on other visitations, depending on where we were campaigning, circumstances would require us to make plays in the huddle. Perhaps our most unusual experience was one Sunday afternoon late in August. I accompanied Ted on his tour of central Massachusetts. He had a busy morning, with drop-ins at breakfasts and cookouts. His was well received for the most part. All together, we hit about eight stops. None of these were places we could call strongholds, but we made some contacts that later in the campaign were helpful. It was just about two o'clock when we finished, and Ted was exhausted and cranky. He growled, "I need to relax and soak in a tub." He asked me to find a tub where he could soak. We were in no-where-land in a small, remote, central Massachusetts town. We suddenly came to a solitary middle-class home. Ted urged me to ask the people if he could soak in their bathroom tub. Sheepishly, I walked up to the door and knocked on it. Almost immediately an older man appeared at the door. Embarrassed, but driven, I asked him if Ted Kennedy could use his bathtub. He misunderstood me. "You mean my toilet?" I said, "No. He would like soak in your tub for a while. He gruffly said, "Is this a joke?" I said, "No. I have Ted out in the car." I pleaded, "It has been a long day; he wants to soak in a tub." Ted got out of the car, briskly walked up to the man and thrust his hand out in a handshake. The homeowner said, "Wow! This is not a joke. Here, let me show you the way." Ted soaked for about a half hour and when he came down he thanked the homeowner and his wife. Everyone smiled. I got the man's name and address and the following week we sent a thank you package of candy. I laugh when I think of that experience.

We worked through the summer based upon the information from the "boiler room." There were big events in Pittsfield and Sturbridge, and we tried to go to everywhere. The "boiler room" information pointed to key individuals who we should keep in touch with, either by mail or phone. We began to build a good enclave of local organizations in the cities and towns, but the McCormack people picked at us every day about debating. When we met on Thursdays, we just temporized and never agreed to do anything.

Late in August, I accompanied Ted and his longtime driver, Jack Crimmons, on a drive through South Boston. We stopped at the Carson Beach bathhouses to say our hellos and try to recruit some voters. Before we were about to leave, Jack ran into one of his friends, Billy Sullivan. Billy asked us if we were spying on our opponent Ed McCormack, pointing across the street to a couple of houses. Jack, truly, said, "No!" Bill retorted, "You couldn't hear the banging? Ed's father, Knocko, is hanging signs in a back yard down that alley." Ted perked up and said excitedly to Jack, "Let's go see Knocko!" We hurried down the alley to a wide-open yard and there was Knocko and a couple other guys making signs for his boy Ed. Ted tapped Knocko on the back and Knocko ignored him. Ted said, "Don't you ever stop?" Knocko returned, "Every time I bang a nail into this sign I envision that I am nailing it into your ass; that thought keeps me going." Ted escaped with, "See ya later, Knocko." Knocko yelled, "Not if I can help it!"

The Debate with Edward McCormack

The radio stations started to catch on that we were trying to avoid a debate; which we were! The reason we were ducking a debate was that some people felt Teddy was not ready to debate. Teddy would spend half an hour every day with a coach – a fellow named Milton Gwirtzman who was a former editorial chairman of the Harvard Crimson – to develop some confidence and key phrases.

McCormack's headquarters was next door to us on Tremont Street, opposite the Boston Common. The McCormack people started to picket our campaign office right away, demanding a debate. At one point Steve Smith said, "Will someone go outside and get rid of those two nerds who are picketing?" Those two nerds were Michael Dukakis and Barney Frank. Right after the Fourth of July we contemplated setting up a debate, so we agreed to meet with representatives from the McCormack campaign to discuss a debate between the candidates. John Dowd and I were assigned to represent Ted's campaign. We would meet once a week with two representatives for McCormack's campaign – Mike Dukakis and Barney Frank. John usually started the meeting by insulting one of them. Then it was my job to do something I can do quite well; talk for a very long time without saying anything of consequence. They were very aggressive about setting up a debate, but we would just string them along until they got frustrated with us. By the end of the meeting, I would suggest we needed another meeting the next week.

The reason we kept delaying was to give Ted time to practice and learn some new debating skills. Finally, Steve Smith said, "I think we are ready now. So, this is what you are going to do. We will debate at South Boston High School, where McCormack went to school." He felt that if Teddy didn't do well, we could chalk it up as being in a very hostile environment.

Finally, I could tell McCormack's people we would debate. This final meeting started as did the others, with John Dowd taking the lead with an insult and I following with a rambling discourse. Then I stopped short and announced, "we will debate in two weeks at South Boston High School. The McCormack representatives were shocked and then relieved it was over.

The newspapers were very much involved and they already agreed to have a panel. It was an interesting debate. Ted and McCormack went back and forth. Considering McCormack's extensive experience with debates and Teddy's lack of experience, Teddy did okay. By the end of the debate, Teddy was furious at McCormack. I was the first one up to Teddy, and I congratulated him and said, "Let's go." He said, "I'd like to go punch him in the nose!" I told him, "You're not going to do that! Let's go!" I moved him quickly out of the auditorium.

We waited for the verdict. The general perception of the public, expressed on radio talks shows, was that Teddy held his own, and if anything, he came off more positive than McCormack. There was no doubt he was a more visibly pleasant person. Those who heard the debate on the radio thought that McCormack won, while those who watched it on television thought Ted won. The TV cameras showed McCormack snarling and grimacing when he talked.

The Primary Campaign

We then switched our focus to a new chapter, which was the primary. Because of the work we had put in all summer, it all started to fall into place. Our campaign began to crank up. Because Ted did well at the South Boston debate, another debate was scheduled two weeks later in western Massachusetts, in Holyoke. It was uneventful because most of the interest and anxiety went into the first debate. Both candidates did okay in Holyoke. It was always expected that Ted would be crushed by McCormack, but he always held his own.

We spent the following weeks gearing up for the primary. Just before the primary, with information from the "boiler room" girls, we found out about an event that was being held for McCormack in North Adams, in Berkshire County. It was a large, regional gathering of Polish Americans, with about four hundred attending – 90 percent of whom were Polish. We were not invited but showed up unannounced. Generally, in Massachusetts, the further you went west the stronger McCormack's support was, especially in North Adams. Despite the rally being for McCormack, the crowd allowed Ted to speak. And it was the most powerful and moving speech I had ever heard Ted give. He concluded his talk with an account of his visit to the site of the World War II Battle of Anzio Beach in Italy. He praised the role of the Polish Legion in that fight. He dramatically finished with reference to the wording on a commemorative tablet placed at the site: "Many of the soldiers of the Polish Legion died in this bloody battle and they lie here. They gave their bodies to Italy; their hearts to Poland and their souls to God." The crowd erupted with thundering applause. With stomping of feet and an explosive applause, echoing, "KENNEDY, KENNEDY, KENNEDY." Until this day, I remember the outpouring of pride and feeling. It was a moment I will never forget.

The gathering in North Adams was a very good indication of how Ted would fare in the primary. Ted did outstandingly well in the primary, beating McCormack two to one. There were a couple of communities where he had some problems, but it was not particularly significant.

Our next focus was the final election, where Ted was running against George Lodge, whose father Henry Lodge was a former United States Senator. Lodge was much more poised, I would say, than Kennedy, but Ted's popularity had soared over the past few months with his victory over McCormack in the primary. Ted beat Lodge rather handedly in the final election, and he became a United States Senator on November 7, 1962, a position he would hold for forty-seven more years.

Ted had offered to pay me for my past and future efforts as his campaign coordinator in Massachusetts. I told Ted that I would have to think about it and that I would get back to him with a response. I had a long discussion with my father, whom I would continuously tap for advice. He asked, "Do you have any money problems?" Somewhat confused, I responded, "Well, no, not really. We just paid off our sofa, but other than that we're doing okay." My father looked at me and said, "Friends don't owe friends anything. You do the best you can to help them. That's what friends are for." From that point on I never accepted a dime from any of the Kennedys for my efforts to help them, no matter the campaign or event. Ted was my friend and I would do anything I could to help him. On the other hand, working for free meant that they really couldn't fire me either.

My Father Edward Doherty and my older brother Edward Doherty - 1934.

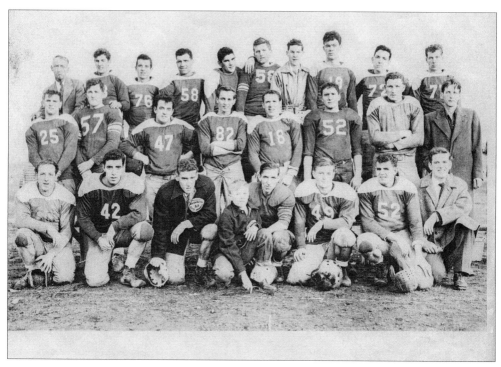

Washington AAs "Washies" City Champions - 1947.

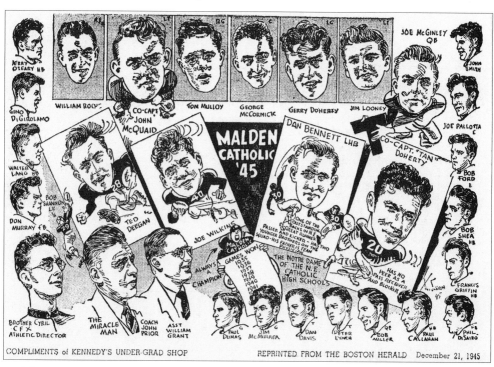

Malden Catholic Football Team - 1945.

Dedication of new Gymnasium Malden Catholic with Marilyn and Gerard Doherty, Brother Cook, Headmaster on the left and Brother Sullivan on the right.

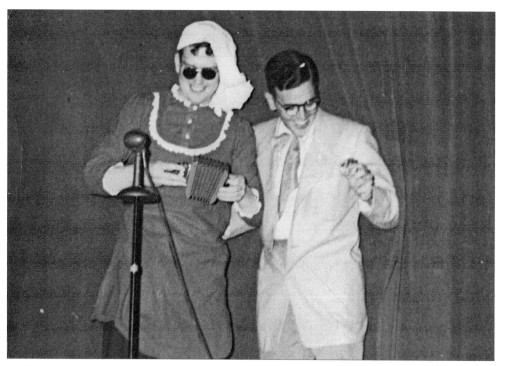

Halloween Show at Trudeau Sanatorium Ted Rummel on the left Gerard Doherty on the right.

TC Ho of Shanghai in the foreground, Gerard Doherty behind Ho, on the right is Paul Palmer and on the left is Carl Zimmer at Trudeau Sanatorium.

Phoenix cottage at Trudeau Sanatorium.

Professor Mowitz on the left front with Classmates at Wayne State University.

Gerard Doherty in office - 1966.

Mowing the lawn at vacation home in Worthington, MA.

The winning candidate, Gerard Doherty - 1956.

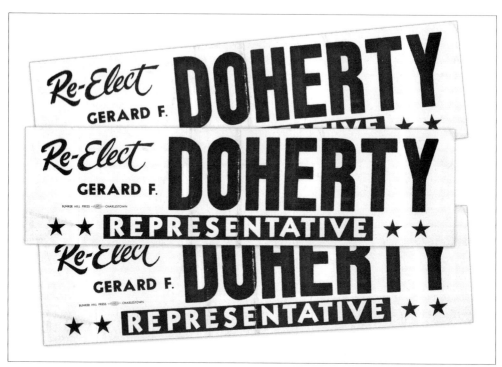

Campaign bumper stickers.

Doherty Campaign Card.

Gerard Doherty with President Kennedy at the Commonwealth Armory dinner in honor of the President October - 1963.

Jacqueline and Senator Jack Kennedy with Charlestown Campaign Workers and Gerard Doherty - 1958.

Gerard Doherty with Jacqueline and Jack Kennedy – re-election - 1958.

Marilyn and Gerard Doherty Campaigning with Ted Kennedy - 1962.

Ted in Stryker Frame with Wife Joan - 1964.

Ted Kennedy campaigning - 1962.

Ted Kennedy campaigning - 1962.

Ted Kennedy campaign in clothing factory - 1962.

Gerard Doherty addressing a House of Representative Commitee.

Representative Doherty receiving award from Boston Fire Department.

Marilyn and Gerard Doherty with Edward Doherty and stepmother Gert Doherty, Joan and Ted Kennedy - 1962.

Gift to Gerard Doherty of Water Color of the Kennedy Compound on Cape Cod – from and painted by Ted Kennedy.

Chapter 3

Post-Election: Giving Thanks

After the election, we celebrated! However, the next day it was back to reality. My job was to close and clean out our campaign headquarters. No heavy lifting really, but it did take some time.

It was the Monday before Thanksgiving and we were still cleaning out the headquarters when Ted Kennedy came by and said, "I want you come with me tonight. I want to find out if you are a fraud or not." Totally bewildered, I looked at him and asked, "What are you talking about?" He then said, "I, Ted Kennedy, am scheduled to have dinner with the prima ballerina of the Bolshoi Ballet tonight at six o'clock at the Hotel Touraine. You are coming with me, if you can." Of course, I could. I called home and I said I would be home later that night. Off we went to meet Maya Plisetskaya, the Bolshoi's star ballerina.

Maya Plisetskaya was a very pleasant and attractive woman and we enjoyed an interesting dinner, discussing a variety of subjects. Halfway through the meal, out of nowhere, Ted Kennedy said, "My colleague here speaks and understands Russian." I thought to myself: this is how he will find out if I have lied all this time about having taught myself Russian at Saranac. He was challenging me. Maya Plisetskaya politely said, "Oh…that's interesting." Ted Kennedy then prodded me, "Why don't you say something to her." To Ted's amazement, I spoke a few words in Russian, such as "My father was a fire-man" and "I live nearby." Maya Plisetskaya, sensing Ted's challenge, knew what I was talking about and graciously responded. After our brief exchange in Russian, she turned to the senator and said, "Your colleague is a well-educated man. He speaks perfect Russian." Teddy groaned in disappointment. I had struggled for the Russian words and used a kind of "pig Latin" Russian. Ted did not know that; Maya did. We all laughed and continued to have an enjoyable dinner.

Teddy asked Maya Plisetskaya, "How long is your troupe going to be in Boston?" She responded, "About two weeks." He then asked, "Do you like America?" She responded, "It is very interesting, and has very worthwhile history." He said, "What I would like, if possible, is to invite you and your troupe to experience a Thanksgiving dinner at my family home on Cape Cod." She was somewhat taken aback. "That's a very kind invitation. Yes, if possible we would like to do that. Whom should I talk to?" He said, "Gerry here will be around tomorrow. You can call him or have one of your associates call him and make arrangements."

The following day, I was working in the empty office of the campaign when Maya's assistant called. We talked about how many people would be coming. She told me there would be twenty-three from the troupe and another four or five associates. We agreed to pick up Maya Plisetskaya and her troupe on Wednesday morning at their hotel. We had two buses. I rode down on one bus. It was a challenge communicating in my version of Russian, but we managed better than I would have expected.

We arrived at the Kennedy Compound and went into Teddy's mother's house. She was there to greet the Bolshoi troupe. Everything was ready for her guests. There were several large dining tables. In the middle of one room, an enormous table was laid out with all sorts of goodies and cheeses. In the middle of the table, there was an enormous punch bowl filled with cranberry juice. The troupe stood in front of the table, cautiously eyeing the bowl. Teddy explained to them how cranberry juice was a traditional drink at Thanksgiving. I turned to a husky looking fellow, who seemed to be in charge of the troupe. Remembering the Russian word for "please" was Пожалуйста, I said it in Russian: "pozhaluista." He took a small cup and scooped some juice from the bowl. After taking a small sip from the cup, he turned to the troupe and said, "сахар," the Russian word for sugar. At that point, all the members of the troupe dove in, filling their cups. So began a delightful, traditional Thanksgiving celebration. It was a welcome respite from the U.S.-Russian tension in those post-Cuban Missile Crisis days.

We had a wonderful time; that day is one of my fondest memories. Of course, it helped that from then on I could kid Teddy, telling him that I had a way with Russians and that, when he gets to be President, he should make me the ambassador to Russia.

State Party Chairman

About a week after the election, Ted Kennedy came to see me. He told me that his brother, the President, was getting a lot of criticism because very little had been done for the Democratic Party by the Democratic State Committee. The President wanted Ted to change that. Ted said that he wanted to make me Chairman of the State Committee.

At the time, the Democratic State Committee consisted of eighty elected members. The State Chairman at that time was the mayor of Somerville, Patrick Lynch. Since I had not been elected to the State Committee, the by-laws precluded my being elected Chairman. On the Friday prior to the meeting to elect a Chairman, the by-laws committee members met and voted a change to the by-laws, which would permit my being elected. Patrick Lynch, a member of the by-laws committee, supported the amendment.

The following Monday, on December eighth, the State Committee met at the Parker House. Everyone showed up. Several people made speeches extolling Patrick Lynch for doing a great job as State Chairman. After giving his farewell speech and thanking everyone, Patrick Lynch resigned. I was nominated. There were five or six people who were very much committed to Edward McCormack who thought that he would be a better fit for the job. However, after a short recess, they came back. The vote was unanimous. I would become the new State Chairman as of the first of the year. My salary would be sixteen thousand dollars a year.

Following my election as State Chairman, I decided not to run for re-election for my seat in the House of Representatives and I resigned at the end of my term. I felt doing both jobs would have been too much for me. Once I assumed my position as State Chairman, I spent the winter months visiting all the cities and towns and ward committees. I was out almost every night. It was very tiring, but very enlightening at the same time. I continued through the winter and then spring came. After getting through the tough winter months, I was starting to have a rather pleasant time. I didn't really have a lot of responsibilities. There were very few meetings during the summer.

Raising Money for President Kennedy

In early July, I got a call from Ted Kennedy. He said, "The Washington people are very, very concerned about my brother, the President. He will be running again in a year, and we must raise some money for him. They think the best place to start raising money is in Massachusetts, so they want the State Committee, namely you and me, to raise the money." He also told me that I was being criticized for being a "do-nothing Chairman." I scratched my head. How can we raise money for the President's re-election campaign? I had no fundraising experience. The only thing I could think of that might be possible was to run a regular banquet "chicken dinner event" to raise money. That is what we decided to do.

We started planning and organizing for the dinner, scheduled for October nineteenth. According to some experts, that would give us enough time to raise the money. I really didn't know anybody who had extensive experience as a fundraiser, so we were pretty much on our own. First, we needed a site. We ultimately decided on the Commonwealth Armory, a Massachusetts National Guard armory adjoining the Boston University campus. It could seat about four thousand people, a very ambitious target. The tickets would cost one hundred dollars. In late August, we began selling tickets. Initially, the demand for tickets was less than overwhelming.

At that point, I was becoming very anxious. The dinner was going to be a flop. When it flopped, Ted Kennedy was going to be embarrassed and my head would be chopped off. That was going to be the end of me.

Rather than wallow in my anxiety, I asked some friends and people on the State Committee to help me out. That is when I had the very good fortune of meeting Bob Fitzgerald, Ted Kennedy's cousin. Bob was a great peacemaker and leader. He just did an outstanding job. Bob's wife, Sally, had been exposed to politics growing up, since her uncle was Paul Dever, Governor of Massachusetts in the early 1950s. She was very outgoing and a great organizer. She and Bob really got involved in the event and worked to make it a success. Another friend, Alice Fitzgerald, who had worked on Teddy's first campaign, came in to volunteer. It was at that time that I met Dick Flavin, who later became a local radio personality. Dick was very talented in public relations and willing to help us. We had about ten or twelve other volunteers in addition to two or three paid workers. We started working to make the dinner a success – with our fingers crossed.

Right after Labor Day, things started to pick up. Then, they began to mushroom. People from across the state were sending money in the mail, over the transom and under the door. We were having difficulty keeping track of them all. By the last two weeks, we had raised approximately five hundred thousand dollars, almost four million dollars in today's purchasing power. The dinner promised to be a huge success. It looked as if we were going to be having a dinner with some five- to-six thousand people!

The prospect of having that many guests presented a number of logistical problems. The main room of the Armory could only hold four thousand people, so we had to expand into the garage attached to the Armory where we could fit another twenty-five hundred. Another problem we had to handle was how we were going to seat so many people in approximately forty-five minutes. We worked out an intricate seating plan where the rows running horizontally, from left to right, were designated alphabetically: A, B, C, D, etc. Rows running vertically were designated numerically: 1, 2 3, etc. Thus, if you had a ticket numbered A50, you would look for Row A, then go down that row fifty tables. We ended up selling approximately sixty-five hundred tickets to the President's Dinner.

When October nineteenth, the day of the dinner, came around, we were finalizing all the arrangements for the evening. At noontime, I was in our headquarters working on the dinner when I got a call. I was told that the President had just arrived in town and he wanted to see me. I was asked if I could meet the President at the Copley Plaza Hotel at two o'clock. I didn't quite know what to expect. At Copley Plaza, I was directed to his room where I was admitted by one of his assistants. The President was sitting at a table. He said, "Gerry, you did a great job. I think we should celebrate!" At which point, he had his aide come in with two dishes of chocolate ice cream. That was our victory meal!

That night, the President came to the Armory in an open limousine in a ten-car motorcade. The streets were lined with people wanting to catch a glimpse and welcome him home. The President relished the reception he received, waving and acknowledging the crowd. Because of the crowds, the motorcade was slowed and the President was late for the dinner.

Nevertheless, the dinner was a colossal success. I was just amazed at the number of people and their enthusiasm. Almost anybody and everybody who was ever a Democrat was there. There were two head tables, one in the main hall and one in the garage. The President presided over the dinner in the main hall; Ted Kennedy presided at the head table in the garage. We were very sensitive that the people who were seated in the garage section have some time with the President. I asked the President if he would have his dessert in the garage, taking Ted's seat at the head table there, and having Ted go to the head table in the main dining hall. That seemed to work out well.

All together it was just a very, very momentous and successful affair. I had to apologize to the President because he had with him an entourage of people and we didn't have any seats for them. He said to me, "Don't worry about it. They are well fed." We ended up having a glorious time. We also raised a lot of money. We were able to give the National Democratic Party a good chunk of it. We kept the rest of the money to continue our work at the State Committee. After that night, everybody could settle down.

Assassination of President Kennedy

We proceeded to go along through the month of November. I was visiting some town committees and had some small, mundane duties. I was meeting with two men who were very helpful during the campaigns. They were both professors – Sam Beer from Harvard and Bob Wood from MIT. Bob Wood later became the head of the MBTA and President of Norwich University. The three of us were sitting in the dinner hall at MIT. It was about two o'clock. We were chatting when suddenly we heard a radio in the background. Everybody gasped; people started to cry. There was the announcement that President Kennedy had just been shot. Stunned and confused, we ended our meeting and went back to the State Committee Headquarters to find out as much as we could. Everyone was just so sad. Even people who were not fond of the President were crying. Those who knew the President personally were distraught. Shortly, we began to make plans for the funeral, trying to be as helpful to the Kennedy family as possible. Governor Endicott "Chub" Peabody allowed me, Ted Kennedy and his aide, Boston Resident Assistant Larry Loughlin, to use the state plane to fly to Washington. We were in touch with a lot people who had worked for the President and who had worked in Teddy's campaign. They were overcome with sadness.

We worked out of Teddy's house amidst a lot of visitors coming back and forth from his house. People were arriving from all over the country. One of the individuals was former Governor of New York, Averell Harriman, who was using Teddy's house as his headquarters. On Sunday, heavy crowds of people waited in line for hours to walk by the casket, which was being held in state at the Capitol. Many of our friends from Massachusetts came down, and some we could help move up in the line. Much of the day was spent talking to people, including dignitaries and celebrities, who wanted to pay their respects but didn't want to wait in line for hours. We tried as best we could to spirit some of them along. In between all that, we were pretty much centered in Teddy's house, doing all sorts of errands to help people. We worked late Saturday and Sunday straight through to Monday helping with the arrangements for the burial on Tuesday. It was just a very sad time for everyone.

Larry Loughlin and I were roommates. We were exhausted. We ate early on Monday night and when we came back to our room we watched football and then fell asleep. About midnight, the phone rang and woke me up. It was Ted Kennedy's secretary, Joe McIntyre. He was a veteran with many years of experience in Washington and had helped Ted with his first term. He was nice enough to stay on; he knew where all the buttons were connected. Joe called to say that there was some sort of altercation at the drugstore next to our hotel. As we came to learn, somebody bumped into an Ethiopian chief of staff and an argument ensued. The Ethiopian reached for his sword and tried to pull his saber out of his scabbard. Someone restrained him. The person involved in the altercation left the area and the Ethiopian Embassy was trying to identify the unknown person. We could provide no information about the matter and went back to sleep.

The next day was the funeral. Larry and I went very early to Teddy's house and helped as best we could. We didn't go to the funeral; we stayed to answer the phone and give people directions. Late that afternoon, Averell Harriman arrived at Teddy's house and was talking with the State Department about the incident of the sword the night before. The State Department was concerned that the Ethiopians were less than happy. However, the whole situation seemed to evaporate by the end of the day. The day concluded and we went to bed early. There was some discussion among the Kennedy family as to whether the President should be buried in Washington, D.C. or in Brookline, where the President was born and raised. Ultimately, the family agreed the President would be buried at Arlington National Cemetery.

Selection of Site for Kennedy Library

When Teddy and I got back to Boston the day after the funeral, he called me and asked me to go with him to the Arnold Arboretum in Jamaica Plain and a few other places to look at sites for a memorial for the President. Coincidentally, in October of 1963, President Kennedy had started to look at sites for a library in his name and came across an ideal spot in Harvard Square, but was killed before plans for the library could get off the ground.

As a help, the state of Massachusetts appropriated three million dollars to buy the site in Harvard Square on which the Charles Hotel sits today, to aid in the Kennedy family's plan to build a memorial library for the President. As negotiations went forward, the neighboring site of the MBTA repair yard was added to make sure the land area for was sufficient for the project. However, before the MBTA site could be acquired, a suitable site for the MBTA repair facility had to be found. That search proved to be very daunting, and the attempt to relocate the MBTA repair facility was eventually defeated.

Area Ten residents, as they were referred to near Harvard Square, slowed down the process of finding alternative sites for the repair yard. There were extensive delays and a special meeting was called for final review. It got very nasty for the proponents of the undertaking; too much traffic, overcrowding of the area, shadows, change of the nature of the community, etc. At first, the thought of a memorial library for the President was welcomed, but now the list of neighbors in opposition was endless. Tempers flared between the proponents of the library and residents as they argued about the changing the tranquility of the local area. After endless speeches of opposition, the meeting closed. The next day Steve Smith, who was the Kennedy family spokesperson and facilitator, met with architects, engineers and developers, and talked about the possibility of a continued search for a more suitable site.

Ted Kennedy who was very frustrated, upset and dispirited, suggested an effort to find an appropriate site for the library without a lot of community opposition. A suggested location was Columbia Point. At first it was similarly dismissed because it was so isolated in Dorchester, but we ended up looking at it further. Someone commented that at night it would sparkle with a multitude of little glimmering lights, explaining to us that the sparkle was caused by ground gas escaping and igniting, due to the site being used as a dump for many years. Ted passed the Columbia Point area on his way to the Cape and he stopped on his own and viewed the largely abandoned site. His interest peaked. Something could be done about the escaping gases; it was handy; there was no opposition; and the view of the harbor was attractive. He talked to a soil engineer who suggested a plan to counter the escaping gas.

Finally, with the Kennedy family's approval, the decision was made to go forward at Columbia Point. This new location at Columbia Point was not chosen until after 1975, with the official groundbreaking of the John F. Kennedy Library not commencing until 1977. An enormous job was to scrap about three or four feet of the surface and replace it with a large layer of a substance like a swimming pool liner. At least that was Steve Smith's description. I spent a couple of weeks getting various local officials' ideas and approvals. He picked the noted architect IM Pei to design the library, and a large New York builder to construct it.

Ted's Plane Crash

Things got back to normal and everyone went back to work after JFK died. Teddy and I went around the state and met with various state committees. Teddy was obviously still very saddened by the loss of his brother. Now, Ted was in his first term as Senator for Massachusetts, I was still State Chairman, and Chub Peabody was Governor. Peabody was very easy to work with. He appointed his personal representative, Bob Cauchon, to work with me at the State Committee. Cauchon was a former naval officer and was very active in Peabody's campaigns. He and I got along very well. However, Peabody faltered on his campaign trail. He kept making all these silly mistakes. A classic was when he said, "I always like to come here to Fall River and visit with my old friends." People in the audience looked a little bit annoyed. Then someone in the back shouted, "You're in New Bedford!" Everybody laughed. That was an example of the well-intended things that he did, but they never came out right. His Lieutenant Governor, Frank Bellotti, was a very able person. He had been elected with Peabody and was a prodigious worker. As time went on, Peabody appeared more and more vulnerable.

By late spring, Bellotti indicated that he would run against Peabody in the Democratic Primary for Governor. Therefore, we had a very intense fight on our hands. Soon it was June and time for the Democratic State Convention. Bellotti had organized many various committees across the state and appeared to be very strong. I was very apprehensive, because if Bellotti won the primary, I would be replaced as State Chairman by one of Bellotti's aides. The day before the convention, I asked Teddy to come up and spend some time here to help Peabody out. Teddy said he would change his schedule and come up a day early. He flew up in a friend's plane with Birch Bayh, who was Senator of Indiana, Bayh's wife and Ted's aide, Edward Moss. They were three miles from the airport in Westfield when their plane crashed. The cause was bad weather. Ed Moss and the pilot did not survive. Senator Bayh and his wife were seriously injured and Teddy was very badly hurt. They transported all of them to the closest hospital in nearby Northampton.

I got to the hospital a little after midnight. Around that time, they couldn't get any of the life signs on Teddy and the doctors thought that his chances of living were very slim. I was there along with a few other people; Maurice Donahue came with me. We waited through the night and it was touch and go. Finally, at about seven o'clock in the morning, they had all of Teddy's vital signs. He had among other things a broken back. By then, the doctors were encouraged and determined that if he continued this path, in all likelihood he would live. Teddy ended up being in the hospital in Northampton for about three months. They gave him a striker frame, which was a cylindrical support that allowed him to lie in the frame with his back to the floor. He would do that for eight hours. Then they would take the equipment, and flip it so that his next position would be him looking straight down. They kept this practice of changing his position for months.

Beginning of Passion for Universal Health Care

About a year prior, Marilyn and I had purchased a home in western Massachusetts in a very small town called Worthington, about sixteen miles from Northampton. During the fall, we would go up there every weekend. On Saturday nights, I would go down to Cooley Dickinson Hospital where Teddy was recuperating, but first I would stop at Friendly's and get him some ice cream. We put a movie picture projector in his room and I would get some films and sit with him as we ate our ice cream and watched the movies. This arrangement went on during the length of his recovery in the hospital. On my visits, we would always get around to healthcare and how the average family could afford it. We discussed my time curing at Saranac Lake. "How did you afford medical treatment, Gerry?" I told Ted how my father, a Boston fireman, was a "string" saver and how we received a little help from Harvard to cover costs, but that my father paid the bulk of the bill. "Now, how do we make health care affordable so that the average person can get the same type of treatment that you and I were fortunate enough to receive?"

Every Saturday evening, after our ice cream and a movie, Teddy and I would revisit this subject. The more we talked about it the more engaged he got. He would ask me how a person in Northampton would pay their bill if they were hit by a car. I would explain that if they had insurance, then the insurance would pay; but if they had no insurance, then the family would have to pay. This would lead to further discussion: If they only have part of the cost, what would happen? If they had no money, what would happen? As I answered, he would say "this is wrong."

On each visit, we returned to the topic and I believe it was the genesis of his life's devotion to universal health care. At the end of the movies Ted would start to tell me about various newspaper articles he had read about a family's health issues and how their neighbors would hold fund raisers for them. These would be stories from all parts of the country. He would always ask, "What if they did not have friends, neighbors or families to help?"

All those conversations between Ted and me about the costs of health care in his hospital room in 1964 focused on the implications for the average American family. He kept coming back to this theme, asking, "How can they afford it?"

I told Ted a story about one of my neighbors, a young girl who had volunteered in his first campaign. She developed kidney problems and, being from a large family, could not afford the necessary treatment. He saw to it that her medical costs were covered without ever talking about it. This was not to be the last time Ted intervened to help someone with health issues who could not afford the needed care.

Ultimately, this dialogue led Ted to say in the 1980 Democratic Convention in New York: "We must not surrender to the relentless medical inflation that can bankrupt almost anyone and that may soon break the budgets of government at every level. Let us insist on real control over what doctors and hospitals can charge, and let us resolve that the state of a family's health shall never depend on the size of a family's wealth"

As the years passed, I watched Ted become much more involved in health care, and particularly universal health care, and to me it was the primary reason he came to be known as the "Lion of the Senate." It was a topic that almost always was included in our conversations over the forty-seven years of our friendship. Often there was a reference back to those Saturday nights in the hospital in Northampton.

Back to Local Politics

While Ted was in the hospital, the 1964 Democratic Gubernatorial Primary took place in September. Chub Peabody was beaten by his Lieutenant Governor, Frank Bellotti. It appeared my whole life would be changed. The general feeling and expectation was that Bellotti was now the head of the party and he should have his own State Chairman. It was just a matter of days before I would be hung out to dry, and I expected it. The night of the primary victory for Bellotti, we were celebrating the election. It was obvious that Bellotti had won and I became the butt of all the gallows comments. Bellotti and his campaign workers were going to either shoot me or hang me. So, I found it only right to go to see Bellotti and tell him that I knew what he was probably going to do, and that I expected it. But I would, if it was helpful, stay on until he appointed a permanent chairman or, if he wanted me to leave immediately, I would do so. I met with Bellotti and he was conciliatory about it, so I went back to the State Committee. After maybe one or two days, Bellotti called me and said that he had a very close friend who he would like to put in as my vice chairman, and that he would work with me on the State Committee. He would effectively run Bellotti's campaign, depending upon what Bellotti needed from the State Committee. The man he appointed was a very good guy, Jack Sheehan, who came from Weymouth. He moved into the State Committee headquarters and we got along fine.

Locally, after the primary, I worked closely with Ed Logue, the head of the Boston Redevelopment Authority, in presenting his community-wide plan to repair and re-engineer the housing stock of Charlestown. Some people might say he was a little on the arrogant side, but he was very talented. He had a tremendous career. He came to Boston and talked about what he was going to do. He and I had our differences. He was going to tear everything down. Logue's plan included demolishing and reconstructing a significant percentage of the existing housing stock in Charlestown. So, for about two years, I was not at all supportive of him. He then decided Boston was a big place and what he needed to do was focus on an area that was manageable. So, he decided to concentrate on Charlestown. At first, I was somewhat belligerent to him. But after a while, what he was doing made sense. He had low-interest funds, which people could get for 2 percent and redo their homes. A lot of people took advantage of it.

After several sessions with the local clergy from all three Catholic parishes – St. Catherine of Sienna, St. Francis de Sales and St. Mary's – we agreed to present the Logue plan to the public. So, in late winter at the Clarence R. Edwards Junior High School, we met a community group of nearly a thousand Charlestown residents. The reception was horrendously bitter. The boos were deafening. The angry response was climaxed with the audience throwing soda cans at the stage. No one had to explain. All of us onstage were belittled and scorned. It was my first time in public supporting the BRA Plan. For weeks, the public anger festered. However, we were able to work cordially with Logue and Charlestown residents years later in the long overdue removal of the elevated train that ran down Main Street.

Campaign Manager for President Johnson

While I was working with Logue, Teddy was still in the hospital, but he was still very concerned that my job as State Chairman would be in jeopardy if Bellotti won the final election. The State Committee's concerns were now focused on the Presidential campaign. Lyndon B. Johnson was heavily favored to win. Unbeknownst to me, LBJ had talked to Teddy a couple of times, and Teddy mentioned my name. Teddy had LBJ announce that I would be LBJ's campaign manager for Massachusetts and the State Committee would run his campaign. As a result, I got to keep my job as State Chairman for the time being. We opened a headquarters near the Boston Common and the amount of foot traffic we had in and out of there was just amazing. We had a lot of people who would come in just for stickers and things like that. Everyone wanted LBJ bumper stickers; we couldn't hold on to them. There was such a run on materials that I finally said, "Why don't we see if we can charge for it." We then started charging a dollar for a bumper sticker, and then we raised the price to two dollars a sticker. Ultimately, we were getting up to five dollars per bumper sticker.

Then the National Committee needed some money to keep going and they looked to us for fundraising. There was a situation where unions couldn't give money directly to LBJ, but they could give money to the State Committee. So, I ended up getting all these moneys from various unions and planned on giving it to LBJ. We even raised a little bit of money of our own for the State Committee. We devised a technique that the unions would give us some money to give to Washington, and some of the money would be used to run the Johnson campaign in Massachusetts. Having all this money, we decided to have a big rally for LBJ at Post Office Square in Boston on October twenty-seventh. The place was jammed. We put up a stage in Post Office Square for Johnson to speak. Afterwards, he stayed around for a couple of hours meeting various people. There was a collective effort on the part of some leading Democrats to try and help Chubb Peabody get a job. One of the leaders of that effort was Maurice Donahue, who was the Majority Leader in the Massachusetts Senate.

My brief encounter with President Johnson confirmed to me his larger than life reputation. It was the last open public rally for a president in Boston, and was a memorable event because of the crowd's enthusiasm and the President's response to it.

After the rally, a small group of twenty met with the President and I found myself facing this six-foot-four President, who inquired about the contents of my hand. When I told him that my hand held donations of eighty-two thousand dollars for the rally, in checks and cash, this huge hand moved swiftly to seize the money out of my hand, and just as swiftly the donations disappeared into his pocket in one smooth motion, without a word. I was not about to challenge the President of the United States.

He didn't know that it was the money we were going to use to pay our bills at the Democratic State Committee. However, we still had some money that was given to us by the unions, although the unions expected that money would go directly to Washington. But the money we raised to keep us afloat, LBJ now had in his pocket. So I held onto the money from the unions.

The National Committee Treasurer, Kenny O'Donnell, was a big Kennedy man. He came from East Boston and played baseball at Harvard. He started hounding me for the money. I kept saying to him, "You already got the money for the President. He put it in his pocket himself." It got to be very stressful, so Teddy had to say something to quiet him down. Kenny O'Donnell's sister, Justine, had been working for him and later, when she came to Boston, had problems finding housing so I helped her find a place to live. We would see her regularly in Charlestown. One night she told me how her brother, the National Treasurer, was very unhappy with me, but I seemed to her like a nice guy. We continued to have a good friendship. Occasionally, she would laugh and say, "They said that you stole eighty-two thousand dollars." I would laugh and hoped that the whole thing would be buried.

A few days later was the election and it seemed to be all LBJ's. He was running against Barry Goldwater. It wasn't even a competition. It was obvious that by the time it came to count the votes on election night, they could just weigh the votes instead. It was a landslide for LBJ. I think it still holds the record for presidential candidates and the portion of votes that they got in a state. That got us through the election.

More State Campaigns: New York, Massachusetts

Around this time, when Teddy's condition had improved, he was transferred to the New England Baptist Hospital in Boston. Incidentally, he was on the ballot for re-election in November, which he won resoundingly with a lot of help from his wife, Joan, while he was bedridden. On top of that, his brother Bobby had given up his position as Attorney General to run for U.S. Senator of New York against the incumbent, Kenneth Keating. During Bob's campaign, his handlers felt that they had enough advisors, thinkers and speech writers, but they lacked a network of experienced street campaigners. As his candidacy was coming up to the last three weeks, his trouble with very few neighborhood campaigns became apparent and worrisome. At one of my visits to Ted at the Baptist Hospital, he asked if I knew any experienced political campaigners that I could send to New York to help his brother, Bob. Since Bellotti had won the Massachusetts Primary for Governor, he had no use for my political friends who had backed Peabody. For example, my own campaign manager, Kevin Kelly from Charlestown, was inactive. He was a former marine, a master organizer and detailed manager. I sent Kevin and a dozen or so experienced Massachusetts campaigners who were not involved with Lieutenant Governor Bellotti's campaign to New York for the last ten days of Bobby's campaign, and they worked very effectively throughout the state.

Robert Kennedy's New York campaign effort mimicked John Kennedy's early election techniques. Going back to JFK's campaign for the House and Senate, one of the standard practices his campaigners employed was distributing a family-themed tabloid to homes in his district about two or three weeks before Election Day. We continued to use this same type of campaign material, which Robert Kennedy was familiar with. However, Robert Kennedy's handlers had no way of providing the customary tabloids, so Ted asked me to get someone who was familiar with the effort. Kevin Kelly had done that type of tabloid for me and for Senator John F. Kennedy's Senate re-election campaign in 1958, and he was delighted to do the same for Bobby. He happily accepted the responsibility of bird-dogging the mass-production printing of Robert Kennedy's tabloid. For three weeks, Kevin worked and slept at the printing shop.

He oversaw the printing and the distribution of the campaign materials to various population centers in the state of New York, such as Buffalo and Palmira, to see that it was done quickly and effectively. It was a terrific challenge, but he succeeded in printing and distributing the appropriate number of publications to all the targeted areas in the state. Obviously, the top priorities were the areas and groups Kennedy's pollsters had determined. Bobby and Teddy were very happy with me and with the campaigners I had dispatched to help with the effort. Bobby ended up winning that election overwhelmingly.

On the night of the New York Senate election, we were back in Boston waiting for the results of the Massachusetts gubernatorial election between Frank Bellotti and John Volpe, a Republican from Wakefield. We had a big gathering in a place a couple of doors down from the State House, and the talk all day was how my head would be chopped off as State Chairman when Bellotti won, which I knew was probably going to happen. The early returns of that night were looking very favorable for Bellotti. The first returns started coming in at about eight-thirty and it seemed overwhelmingly clear that he would be Governor. At about nine o'clock I was getting ready to leave; I couldn't take any more comments about how I was going to be hung by Bellotti. Then the returns came in from Lawrence and it was very unusual. It broke the whole steady stream of Bellotti victories. Volpe carried Lawrence! More returns came in. Then Volpe started carrying the intermediate sized cities. I was hopeful, but it still appeared that Bellotti would win. I went home, went to bed and woke up about six o'clock in the morning. The returns had them almost at a dead tie, but by 10 a.m. Volpe ended up beating Bellotti by about twenty-three thousand votes.

We didn't have a Governor who was going to fire me, so I would still be the State Chairman!

That day, when I went to visit Ted at the hospital, RFK was there. Ted had told him that I had sent all those helpers to New York. RFK knew about the distribution of the tabloid and our two dozen Massachusetts organizers. Robert Kennedy thanked me and asked me to express his appreciation to all the Massachusetts volunteers.

I had become very friendly with Bellotti's representative, Jack Sheehan, and decided that I would ask if he would continue to work at the State Committee even though Bellotti lost. There were rumblings from some leftover people from the State Committee, who always thought I was less than great and who, over the years, had problems with the Kennedys. It got a little wobbly until John McCormack, who was Speaker of the House at that time, held a press conference. McCormack stood up and made things clear, saying: "My State Chairman is Gerard Doherty and I will support him! Anyone who does not want to support him can go someplace else." So, there it was; I was assured of staying on the job. It was still very difficult, as people continued to have their doubts about me.

In late January 1965, I had an assistant by the name of Andy Vitale who had worked for Kennedy through all his various campaigns. He came from western Massachusetts. It was wintertime when we ran out of money at the State Committee, so we had to raise some money. People were tired of the old rubber chicken dinners we had used so often to raise money. By coincidence, Vitale came back one morning at about eleven o'clock and said, "I'm sorry I'm late. I had breakfast with a fellow I went to prep school with and he's in Boston working on something very interesting. He represents film producers and is

trying to get a theatre to have the first showing of a movie."
Vitale explained to me that the movie was about an Austrian
family who were singers. We agreed to use this movie premier
as a fundraiser.

First, we had to borrow some money to reserve the theater
for its first showing, which cost us ten thousand dollars. It
sounded more interesting than the State Committee trying to
raise money with the typical rubber chicken dinner, yet a lot of
people thought I was out of my mind. It was the first time anyone had a fundraiser and used a movie as the attraction. With a
lot of effort, we sold the tickets. A lot of people were very hopeful we would be successful. The day of the function, at about
eleven o'clock in the morning, we seemed to be in good shape.

Andy came in and said, "I did something I hope you think
is okay?" I said, "I'm sure whatever you did was in our best
interest." Andy said, "I was in the hotel and I saw these women
in Tyrolean costumes. An older woman, a younger woman, and
a young girl. And I said to them, 'Are you in town for the
movie?' They responded, 'No, what movie? We have a place in
Vermont but we are here for an antique and craft show.' Puzzled, I said, "I thought you were here for the movie tonight? It's
the *Sound of Music*. It's about the Von Trapp family.' They
looked surprised and startled and said, 'We are the Von Trapps.'
Surprised, I said, 'I am running an event and would like you to
come as my guests tonight.' So, I invited them to the show at
the Metropolitan Theater."

We had an almost a full house that night. The theater held
forty-two hundred seats. We had great success selling the tickets for the ground floor seats, and the first balcony also sold
pretty well. The second balcony was a tough sell, but overall
there was surprising support. Ted Kennedy was pleased with

the enthusiastic response. The movie was outstanding. At inter-
mission, Ted Kennedy got up and spoke, saying: "We have a
very special surprise! We have Maria von Trapp and her two
daughters with us tonight." At that point, the applause was thunderous! It was a very successful night and people were very
complimentary to me and Andy about being so resourceful and
imaginative in raising money. Altogether, the evening was a
tremendous social, political and financial success.

Later, in March of 1965, there was a special election for a
State Senate seat in Brookline. Our friend, Representative Beryl
Cohen, ended up beating out a woman who was a Republican
choice, Freyda Koplow. It was a very intense fight. The day of
the election it was an unusually rainy day. Republicans always
vote in the rain and in the middle of the afternoon. However, I
had developed good relations with the unions in and around
Boston. We needed a lot of help and I must say that we got all
the union people very involved. They sent us door knockers and
drivers and they got their phones going. It was just a miraculous
thing! In my many years in politics I never witnessed such an
effective effort to get people out to vote. People who had not
voted were pinpointed; we had countless volunteers going door-
to-door, and a battery of phone calls were made between the
hours of three and eight o'clock. We pulled out an enormous
vote and ended up winning the fight. I remember, for example,
a woman friend say, "All day, all I did was answer the phone or
the door; I kept getting interrupted to go out and vote. Finally,
I screamed at one of the volunteers who knocked at my door, 'I
have been trying to get dressed to go and vote for over an hour,
but I have to keep answering the phone and the door.'" She

came out and we had a driver take her to the polls to vote. Everybody was surprised and it made my life a lot easier that they thought I knew, for the first time, what I was doing.

Around the summer of 1965, we were living from hand to mouth at the State Committee. We had some financial problems and ended up having a benefit at the Wilbur Theatre, where Mary Martin and Dennis O'Keefe were starring in a play called *Jenny*. On a risk, we bought the show and ended up filling it. Everyone was very pleased with the performance and I got a lot of people off my back.

Frank Morrissey Judgeship Nomination

In the fall of 1965, my longtime friend from Charlestown, Frank Morrissey, was sponsored by Ted to become a federal judge. He had been a longtime friend of the Kennedys, especially Ted's father, Joseph P. Kennedy. Shortly after LBJ's election in 1964, LBJ had a conversation with Ted's father who was very ill. Mr. Kennedy asked if LBJ would appoint Frank Morrissey, who had been an almost personal aide to Mr. Kennedy for over thirty-five years, as a federal judge. The President happily honored the request and presented his request for Frank to be elevated to the Federal District Court in Boston.

Ted Kennedy over the years had been friendly with and dependent on Frank to visit him and help with his constituent needs. Robert Kennedy also concurred with the Morrissey selection. Everything went along smoothly until Everett Dirksen, Senator of Illinois, registered his opposition to the appointment. The Boston Globe began to write a series of criticisms about the Morrissey choice, indicating that his background qualifications were attracting controversy. Ted was out of the country visiting U.S. soldiers in Vietnam when his supposed good friend, Senator Joseph Tydings of Maryland, also expressed his opposition to appointing Frank. The Boston Globe berated Morrissey. His resume indicated his undergraduate training was done at the Staley College of the Spoken Word. That background was suspect by national and local newspapers. Coming under scrutiny was his law school background. Supposedly, he received his legal training at a school in Atlanta, Georgia, which no longer was in existence. No one could be found who could validate his story. The Boston Globe was merciless in assailing his qualifications. When Ted returned from Vietnam, it was clear, despite LBJ's support, that the Morrissey nomination was hopeless. Consequently, almost immediately after his return from Asia, Ted personally went to the floor of the Senate and withdrew the Morrissey nomination.

I had been in Washington for weeks and when I returned an almost unbelievable thing occurred. A fellow I was in the legislature with had become a district court judge and served in the state court system in Boston with Frank Morrissey. His name was Judge Frank Foster. Just when I returned, he called me and volunteered that he had bundles of mail for Frank Morrissey. I picked it up and looked through the voluminous pile. An office assistant helped me read and categorize the bags full of mail. Accidently, we found a letter from a fellow by the name of Crowley. His letter to Frank wrote about their days together in law school in Georgia. It was cruel fortune. If it had only been found sooner Frank's story would have been credible and events would have been different. It would have had a happy ending.

Leaving Politics to Start Law Practice

In the beginning of that summer, I was asked by Ted to go to breakfast at his home at Three Charles River Square. Also at the meeting were Tip O'Neil, Congressman Ed Boland and Maurice Donahue, who was President of the Massachusetts Senate. Boland was Maurice Donahue's cousin. After breakfast, Ted Kennedy led the discussion. He had access to a newly conducted gubernatorial poll, which showed that Attorney General Ed McCormack was leading Maurice Donahue by fifteen points. Speaking as a longtime friend, Ted spoke directly to Maurice and said, "You can't win and I don't want to see you embarrassed." Maurice quickly stood up and said, "I thought you were my friends," and abruptly left. That afternoon I went to see Maurice in his Senate President office. He greeted me, saying: "You were the only one at the table who really is my friend." He was more hurt than angry at that morning's event. I weakly tried to encourage him, "It's still early and things might change." He continued planning his effort for the early fall pre-election. About a month after that meeting, a senator who was a Maurice supporter came by my office at the Democratic State Committee to chat about Maurice's prospects of winning. She sat opposite me and said, almost embarrassingly, "Jerome," (she always called me Jerome), "Turn your head and look out the window." I did what she wanted, and then very seriously and softly she advised me: "Jerome, success in politics is a lot like sex. To be successful you must excite people. Maurice doesn't arouse anyone except his closest friends."

As State Chairman, I was supposed to be neutral but at every turn I was criticized for being too partial to Maurice's campaign. At rallies, conferences, dinner events, my partiality for Maurice was evident. That summer, Maurice ran in the primary and lost the Democratic nomination for governor to Edward McCormack, as the poll that Ted referenced at his house had indicated. After McCormack won the nomination I tried to help him, but I wasn't too welcome. I was greeted with suspicion because I was Maurice's friend.

We then went back to the State Committee and continued to struggle along. I had told Ted Kennedy that I would like to leave and that there were of a lot of problems. Also, I had a salary of sixteen thousand dollars but I wasn't paid for a year and a half. It was starting to drain on me. Finally, in 1967, Teddy said, "I have somebody to take your place." He was a lawyer by the name of Lester Hyman who worked as Governor Peabody's secretary. I wished him well.

After I left my position as Democratic State Committee Chairman in late January 1967, my good friends Senator Bill Bulger and former Senator Jim Hennigan gave me a small office in their suite at 73 Tremont Street. The first month back at my law office I learned the difference between grossing and netting. All together I made sixty-eight dollars for the month.

At my new law practice my good friends supported me. Elinore Shiels, a woman I worked with at the State Committee, came to work as my assistant at the law firm. At the time, I told her I could not afford to pay her. She said, "I'll take my chances and I'll work as a volunteer." I said, "For three months we will do the best we can. If at the end of three months, we aren't making it, you will have to leave." Almost immediately, there was a knock at the door and there was a short fellow, whom I knew a little bit about, who wanted to help and contributed some money over the years. He was from New York, and was an architect's representative. Incidentally, his name was Bob

Doherty. He came in and he talked to me about how he was going to be more active in New England and how he wanted to retain me without making bones about it. He opened his wallet and gave me a check for four thousand dollars for the first month. It was unbelievable; it was like Christmas. Bob Doherty, Herbert Hoffman and I scheduled a meeting in late February with Ted Kennedy and a few other legislators. Teddy was getting a lot of great headlines. Everyone was excited to see him. We met in a big room at the Ritz Carlton and, after twenty-five minutes of hearing how great we all were, this Bob Doherty got up and made a speech. He said, "It's great to make speeches, but I believe in putting my money where my mouth is. Today I gave the Chairman some money and I think that everyone in this room should start to give money so that he can feed his family." It was both amazing and embarrassing, but very successful.

I first became acquainted with Herbert Hoffman when I became Chairman of the Massachusetts Democratic State Committee in 1962. His family owned and operated a clothing factory in a building at the Boston end of the Charlestown High Bridge. Herbert Hoffman had been a Boston University graduate when he took over the management and manufacturing of his family business after his father's untimely death. He manufactured work clothes under the names of Built Well and Double Wear. At his onset, Herbert was predicted to bankrupt the company within a year. Instead, he surprised everyone with his effort and the company began to prosper with the making and selling of their work clothes. After about a year or so Herbert had become an unanticipated success.

A bigger surprise was his purchase, together with the Herald newspaper owners, of rights to a TV station, known today as Channel 5, after an intense fight with The Boston Globe. Supposedly, there was some skepticism that Senator John Kennedy aided in the selection process and in return received a Nobel Prize for his book *Profiles in Courage*, for his behind-the-scenes efforts in helping Herbert Hoffman and the Herald acquire the TV station.

When I got elected to the legislature in 1956, one of my political friends, Jim O'Halloran, owned a building next to the Hoffman building. O'Halloran was very supportive of my efforts to raise money for the Democratic Party. Because of Jim O'Halloran, Herbert Hoffman was always willing to help me financially and politically. Our friendship extended for over sixty years. Herbert enjoyed success in both business and real estate.

About the time when I was getting out of formal politics, Herbert and I got into the cable antenna TV business together. In the mid-sixties, Herbert asked me to help him to promote a business. There was a process popularly known as CATV or Cable Antenna Television. It was a technique of communication that would enhance both coverage and reception of TV. Simply put, it was a process of stringing receptor cables along poles scattered around cities and towns. Hoffman's group had acquired licenses to string up the cable in about fifteen cities and towns surrounding Boston. As I recall, these licenses were part of a master entity, New England Cable Vision. Congressman Torbitt McDonald announced that these cables had to be up and running and effectively able to transmit visual pictures for the operating entity to be validated. Malden was his hometown so that's where we started. Ultimately, when the system was up and running, our operation was recognized as a legal operating entity. Several months later, the Warner Community Cable Company purchased our entity. I had a small stock interest in it and I went on to other things.

At the outset of my involvement in the cable company, I met a fellow named Peter Doelger who had a small stock option in our enterprise. In 1975, an international conflict occurred between the United States and the Middle East, a major supplier of oil to the United States. The United States suffered a fuel crisis. Gasoline was rationed. There was a bizarre form of rationing. For example, if your license plate ended in an odd number you could only buy gas on an odd numbered day. Furthermore, to conserve fuel usage, the universal speed limit was reduced from sixty-five to fifty-five miles an hour. This limitation was carefully policed by the law enforcement authorities.

The authorities also required each state to establish an energy control agency, which promulgated rules for use and distribution enforcement. Energy conservation was strictly enforced. To aid in this universal supervision and reduction of energy conservation, each state developed a comprehensive plan for both residential and commercial consumption. The state of Massachusetts, through the legislature, developed a system to diminish home and commercial use of cooling and heating measures. To more effectively monitor this, the state was divided into four spheres of supervision. For example, the southeast part was centered on the greater Fall River area.

Fortunately, the state senator for much of that area was Senator Tom Norton of Fall River. That area, like all others, advocated for service groups to help plan for effective consumption. Peter Doelger, together with a fellow named Gerry Regan, were two of the few respondents with experience that responded with their company DMC, Design Management

Corp. Their efforts were designed to make home visits and recommendations to residents about energy consumption features. These were things like eliminating drafts from windows and door frames, reducing water flow when flushing toilets, and changing leaking faucets. These service calls were at a minimal cost of ten dollars. However, the challenge was to find enough reliable workers to carry out these home and commercial visits. The Doelger group and I were able to solve this problem. My father was a fireman, my cousin was a fireman. In addition to them, I knew a lot of other firemen. Most of them, by experience and development, were handymen, and their work schedules gave them a lot of stagnant time to do side work. Therefore, we gathered an army of firemen who could carry out these home visits on their days off. At the end of the first quarter, the southeastern group had serviced more homes than the other three regions combined. Consequently, Doelger's group began to take over other sections of Massachusetts to accomplish the goal of consumption control.

Over the next several years of great success and good fortune, the company was sold to a large utility group in the Midwest. We were compensated a good amount of money for our holdings. In the interim, I was busy at my law practice. In 1967, The Boston Globe had publicly supported Ed Logue's campaign for mayor. They felt that he was the strong candidate against the popular Louise Day Hicks, who arose in the aftermath of busing. Kevin White's candidacy was a surprise, but his victory was more of a surprise. On primary election night, Ted Kennedy watched the returns at my home in Charlestown. As soon as White was declared the winner, Ted had me call Kevin White and congratulate him. When Ted spoke to Kevin, Ted seemed to frown, mumbled something and said, "Gerry, you talk to him." I spoke to Kevin. He seemed cold and, almost bluntly, said he was broke and hoped Ted would raise money for him. The call was shortly terminated. Ted looked quizzically at me and said, "He seems very cold. What do we do now?" I said tersely, "We raise him some money!" Shortly after that we had a fundraiser at a hotel and we gave White fifty thousand dollars. Kevin very soberly thanked me. After that he beat Louise Day Hicks whom all the Boston newspapers opposed. Ted Kennedy's relationship with the new mayor was polite, at best.

Kevin White had been very friendly with Ed McCormack and when McCormack announced his campaign for U.S. Senator, White pledged his support. He made it clear he was supporting Ed McCormack. To his credit, White's loyalty never wavered. After Ted's victory in 1962, Kevin's relationship was cordial and prudent. However, even though I had raised funds for Kevin, he was still cool towards me. His people made it clear as long as I stayed out of Boston, I would be left alone.

Gerard F. Doherty

Chapter 4

Robert Kennedy Campaign in Indiana

On March 16, 1968, Robert Kennedy announced his candidacy for President. The following Monday I called Ted and left a message saying I was willing to help his brother in any way possible. On Thursday, I was having lunch at the Parker House. Unexpectedly, the waiter brought over a phone and said, "Senator Ted Kennedy would like to speak to you." Our conversation was one-sided. He thanked me for my earlier offer to help his brother. He quickly got to the point. The first state that Bobby might run in was Indiana, due to how little time he had. They were inaugurating their first Presidential Primary the following Thursday and paperwork for participation had to be filed. Ted asked if I knew anyone in Indiana. I said, "No." Or if I knew anyone who was familiar with politics there. I said, "No." It was obvious that he wanted to get a more positive response about the details of running there, but more importantly the process of getting on the ballot. He did not ask me to go. Reading his mind, I said, "Ted, do you want me to go?" He said, "Yes!" And he added that RFK Headquarters in Washington had all the information I would need. They gave me three names: Michael Riley, Lou Mahern and Bill Schreiber. Michael

Riley was an attorney in Indianapolis. Lou Mahern was a Democratic activist who later became a member of the Indiana Senate, and Bill Schriber was a Democratic activist.

I met these three men at the airport in Indianapolis after flying from Washington around seven o'clock on a Thursday night. From there, we went to Michael Riley's office in downtown Indianapolis. For two hours, I was briefed about the specifics of Indiana elections. First, to solidify a candidate's name on the Presidential Primary Ballot for nomination, the candidate had to submit fifty-five hundred valid signatures of registered voters of the party whose nomination was sought. Also, you had to provide no more than one thousand voters from a single congressional district for appropriate filing. There were eleven congressional districts, two of which were in Indianapolis, restricting a candidate to two thousand appropriate signatures in Indianapolis. The remainder of the signatures had to be obtained in the remaining nine congressional districts. Obviously, we had to concentrate on where the most voters were, like South Bend and Fort Wayne. We enlisted young people from the various universities across the state, such as the University of Indiana, which provided us a large student corps to help us with the signature gathering.

The challenge was getting all the required signatures and then submitting their names to the various election departments across Indiana for certification by the following Thursday. At Riley's office, we talked about how to accomplish our task in the six days we had left. We stayed in Michael Riley's office until nearly one o'clock in the morning devising a plan of action. We had a list of all the colleges and universities, and assigned each respective college to one of the appropriate local congressional districts. We also sketched out a list of Catholic high schools in urban areas and worked out other high priority areas. We then dispersed and came back to Riley's office at 6 a.m.

We then had a list of the best sources for prospective helpers. The first individual was a seminarian in Fort Wayne. His name was Joe Kelly. He agreed to help and enrolled some of his friends. The next call reached a fellow in Kokomo. He was puzzled how we got his name, but nevertheless agreed to help. As we made calls from 7 to 9 a.m., Lou Mahern had already secured a sample ballot with Indiana Governor Roger Branigin's name listed as a candidate. Lou asked his friend, a printer, to remove the governor's name and to replace it with Robert Kennedy's and to print a few thousand copies. We then started to distribute the new petitions with Bobby's name across the state via Greyhound buses. Amazingly, things went very well.

The First Congressional District, Gary, was close to Chicago. It had a tough political organization to crack. Someone gave me the name of a professor at the University of Chicago, Richard Wade. He said he would help recruit supporters in the city. In a matter of minutes, he called back and gave me the name of a young woman, Grace Ann Barry of Chicago, who could be helpful. She turned out to be a superstar. Within a few hours, she had a bus load of volunteers who would gather signatures in Gary.

We discovered a problem: someone from the governor's office staff was interrupting some of our deliveries of the Kennedy nomination papers that were sent by bus. That occurred at about one o'clock. However, most of the cities in the state already had received their election materials uninterrupted. As our massive delivery operations were underway, we went for breakfast next to Riley's office. I ordered pancakes because I hadn't eaten since noon the day before. Still tired, I was not paying attention to my meal and dropped a syrup-laden pancake on my lap. After an energetic effort to clean the massive stain on my light gray slacks failed, I left the breakfast place and placed a local newspaper over the front of my pants to cover the messy stain.

As we were walking back to Riley's office we encountered a stream of high school students on the next block. Many of them were wearing sweatshirts with "Crispus Attucks" printed on the front. I questioned Michael about it, and he said that it was the name of the high school on the next block. When we got back to his office, I asked him what he knew about the school. All he said was there were a lot of students there and they had a good basketball team. I asked Michael if he could get the principal on the phone for me. Almost immediately, I was connected to the principal. I mentioned how I was familiar with name "Crispus Attucks" because in 1770, during the Boston Massacre, Attucks, an African American, was the first civilian killed by British soldiers. I commented on the coincidence of my coming from Boston to help Robert Kennedy and encountering students from his school. I told him the purpose of our trip to Indianapolis. I mentioned that Robert Kennedy was going to the State House the following Thursday to file his nomination papers. I invited the Crispus Attucks' band to lead our planned parade to the State House where Kennedy would file his papers for his candidacy for President of the United States. The principal got very excited and said it would be a great honor.

Back at Riley's office, we worked very effectively. We already had enthusiastic workers in all parts of the state. It was a daunting challenge to get the eleven thousand-plus signatures filed with the appropriate city, county and town clerks, and get them certified as necessary. Our signatures had to be appropriately spread across the state, then they had to be gathered, verified and brought to the State House by eight o'clock the following Thursday evening.

That afternoon at about three o'clock, I had a Machiavellian idea. I called the principal at Crispus Attucks and told him that his school band's appearance with Robert Kennedy at the State House might have to be canceled. He sadly asked why. I told him about the difficult chore of getting the necessary signatures, within the time constraint, for Robert Kennedy and how it was an almost impossible feat. He was disappointed. I told him how we were desperately working to get the necessary signatures, organizing everywhere to achieve our task. Then I said, "But I have an idea, which would be enormously helpful. Do you think we could get some of your young band members dressed in uniform to stand in front of all the black churches tomorrow night to gather signatures?" He quickly responded, "Yes, of course. My kids will love it!" I told him that we would work out the details.

I learned that Saturday night was a busy church night in Indianapolis. In the black communities, mostly women made up the large congregations and a remarkable number of them turned out to be registered voters. We gathered over two thousand valid signatures outside the churches. We also recruited a great number of women volunteers.

Late Saturday evening, I met Reverend Joe Brown. Somehow, he found us working out of Michael Riley's office. He was very laid back. No one seemed to know much about him but he offered to contact the black clergy around the city. He took a stack of papers and went off to do his own thing, whatever that was. Michael Riley and I visited twelve black churches that evening. It was amazing to see the band members nattily dressed in uniform in front of the churches. I introduced myself to several church officials, who remarked about the band members standing outside. They were mostly women, and, remarkably, all friends of Reverend Joe Brown. All of them were excited to help.

On Sunday, we had judiciously placed volunteers to stand about a block away from the Catholic and Protestant churches. As people passed, the band members very politely solicited churchgoers to sign nomination papers. It was stressed that our volunteers respectfully ask churchgoers for signatures. It was very subtle and orderly. Sunday afternoon I went to Michael's office, which had become our communication center. We called people around the state and found them busy collecting signatures. We then, later in the afternoon, developed a set of plans about how on Monday our workers could go to city, county or town halls and get the signatures certified. We instructed this faceless army of eager helpers what their next task would be.

Confronting County Clerk: Later a National TV Star

One district that gave us problems was Gary, which was in Lake County. The clerks in Lake County opposed Robert Kennedy and pledged their loyal support to Governor Branigin by refusing to certify RFK's nomination papers. The governor had a stronghold on all government workers. We learned that state and city employees in Indiana who received patronage jobs had to give 2 percent of their salary back to the Democratic Party, so very few wanted to jeopardize their jobs by helping the governor's opponent. This was the main reason that the entire Congressional delegation, except for Senator Vance Hartke, did not support Bobby's campaign. Although a few did help surreptitiously.

Nevertheless, I got on the telephone and called the assistant clerk who oversaw the actual certification process. She adamantly refused to start the process so I brought my Irish temper into play and told her what I would do, in the hope that she would be intimidated. The assistant clerk still refused to budge. I tried once more and again failed to move her. Later in life, I did meet the assistant clerk under very different circumstances. I was president of the board at the Kennedy Library and the former assistant clerk was the honored guest and speaker at an event. Jane Pauley and I buried the hatchet and enjoyed the evening together.

Ultimately, we had to hire a lawyer to get a writ of mandamus to order the clerks in Lake County to certify nearly twenty-five hundred of Robert Kennedy's nomination signatures. Even the lawyer we hired cited his support of the governor, but he agreed that what the clerks were doing was wrong, so he represented us and resolved the situation in our favor.

Confronting Robert Kennedy Washington Staff

I was called by Robert Kennedy headquarters on Sunday night and asked to return to Washington for a meeting the next morning. I arrived to the meeting late. There were already about eight people in the room, including Ted Sorenson, Larry O'Brien, Kenny O'Donnell, Steve Smith and others. As was the case with Ted Kennedy's Washington staff, many viewed me as an outsider who had too much power and was possibly a threat to them. It was immediately apparent that the sense of the group was that Indiana was not the best place to start Bob's campaign. As I was the new kid on the block and an apparent threat to some, I did not have any voices of support for my efforts in Indiana. It was pointed out that in the 1960 Presidential Campaign, Indiana was President Kennedy's poorest showing of all the industrial states, where he lost by more than two hundred thousand votes. Coupled with that fact the State Democratic Party was supporting Governor Branigin, I sensed that a decision was already made by the group to skip Indiana.

Steve Smith, Robert Kennedy's brother-in-law, was somewhat apologetic in his comments because he knew I had spent four days working very hard for Bobby; however, he agreed with the others in the room. The negative feeling was overwhelming. I was surprised and almost beleaguered, but I politely modified my anger when I said. "I have just spent four sleepless days out there. As Ted knows. I am not an optimist. I am a realistic conservative. We will have over eight thousand validated signatures filed at the State House by Thursday of this week and we will have a crowd of several thousand at the State House in Indianapolis that night. The response we have gotten from the people in Indiana is overwhelming. Bob can win there. I think it would be a grave mistake if he did not run in Indiana. It would display a defeatist attitude on his national campaign." A minute of silence followed, and then the door of the meeting room opened. Robert Kennedy walked in, made a couple of perfunctory hellos, and said, "How is it going?" Steve Smith responded, "Gerry just came back from Indiana and reported he will have enough signatures to get you on the Indiana ballot this Thursday night." Steve continued, "But most of us think it would be a mistake and it would have a disastrous effect on your overall campaign." Bob turned to me and asked my opinion. I gave him a short but definite opinion. "You would win there. In four days, I and hundreds of volunteers have gathered close to eight thousand signatures to qualify you to be on the ballot." As I was about to continue, Bob interrupted me. "If I am as good as I think I am, then I will win in Indiana. But if I am not as good as I think I am, I should find out sooner rather than later. So, I am going to run in the tough state of Indiana."

Campaign in Indiana Resumes: Family Joins

On Thursday, March 28, RFK flew from Columbus, Ohio, into Indianapolis to officially enter the campaign for President. He made a few comments to the enthusiastic crowd of several thousand people who crowded around the State House. Kennedy gave a short speech. "If I can win in Indiana, I can win in every other state." He asked the gathered Hoosier crowd to help and they roared in support.

Kennedy and his party went to downtown Indianapolis to the Hotel Marriott to make a few brief comments to the press. "I am not running against Governor Branigin. I consider him an outstanding governor and a friend. I am running for president." RFK was certified as a valid candidate and the campaign was officially on!

On the weekend of March 30, Ted was in town. He met with our local group of supporters for an upbeat and positive informational session. Sunday, we campaigned around Indianapolis. That afternoon we had a big meeting of volunteers.

Something everyone who spent any time traveling by car with Senator Kennedy discovered was that he was a world class backseat driver. On one occasion, we were both heading to the Cape for different reasons and he asked if I could drive him, which I agreed to do. As soon as we got outside of Boston he asked me to pull over so he could drive. Apparently, I was taking the wrong route.

During one of our visits to Indianapolis we were scheduled for a meeting on the other side of the city, so I asked one of the young volunteers to drive us. Once under way, Ted, who was sitting in the back seat, was a constant chatter of "go left…watch out on the right…can't you find a better route?" Finally, the young man pulled over, turned to the senator and said, "Senator, why don't you drive and I will sit in the back?" Ted demurred and we finished the ride in silence. It became increasingly difficult to get volunteer drivers.

Later that afternoon we had a tea reception featuring Rose Kennedy, Bob's mother. There were close to one thousand enthusiastic women gathered with her. Early in the evening we had more meetings with various ethnic groups. After a long day, Ted and I adjourned to my room at the Hotel Marriott, ordered club sandwiches and turned on the TV at eight-thirty. As we started to eat, LBJ was on television and he announced that he would not run for re-election for another term. Both of us were stunned and amazed. Ted said, "let's get busy and check around." He got on the phone with Bob, and an instantaneous plan was formed. Ted would call around the country to friends, governors, and mayors asking them for their support and to join Bob's campaign. For about two hours he made a litany of calls to fellow senators, big city mayors, and important fundraisers. Most of the individuals reached were surprised, but for the most part were non-committal. We stopped calling just after midnight. It was not a particularly positive canvass.

RFK started his campaign in Indiana on April fourth. He made a series of stops in downtown Indianapolis, then to Notre Dame in South Bend and Ball State College in Muncie. At Notre Dame he spoke to a crowd of five thousand, where he focused on the plight of the impoverished.

Bill Foley and Kevin Leary, both from Boston, were RFK's advance men when he went to Ball State. Before Robert Kennedy could go, Bill and Kevin had to make sure the Muncie airport was large enough to land RFK's airplane. In fact, the runway was too small so Bobby had to switch planes before making the flight from South Bend to Muncie. When RFK arrived, he proceeded in a motorcade to Ball State, where he spoke to the crowd of twelve thousand that filled the basketball gym. There wasn't an empty seat in the house. The crowd expanded onto the gym floor and right up against the stage where RFK was speaking. I remember the scene; it was a mob of excited supporters. People were clawing and scratching at a chance to touch Bobby and his wife.

By the time we got out of the gymnasium to get Bobby back to his plane, he had swollen hands with scratches all up and down his arm and he had missing buttons on his shirt cuffs. The crowd was tremendous.

<u>Martin Luther King Assassinated</u>

After Kennedy finished his speech at Ball State and before he got on his plane to leave, he was informed that Martin Luther King had been shot in Memphis. Kennedy flew back to Indianapolis to kick off a rally in the African American area to spur local voter registration. The minority community was excited that Kennedy's first major appearance was scheduled in their community. Early that evening, when news had broken that King had died, Mayor Richard Lugar called me and asked me to cancel Kennedy's appearance for public safety reasons. Michael Riley heard Lugar say, "If Kennedy chooses to speak, he does it at his own risk." Kennedy canceled going to headquarters downtown and chose to head straight to the rally. On the way, he scribbled some notes.

The speaking site was very dark, with little lighting. There were thousands waiting for Kennedy to speak. Upon his arrival, the debate continued as to whether he should speak. Congressman John Lewis argued that somebody had to speak to the crowd that had been waiting for over an hour, especially given the circumstances of King's death. It was a majority African American crowd of thousands. It was finally agreed that the rally would go on and Bobby would speak.

Kennedy got up to speak in the flatbed of a truck, "I have sad news for you and for all of our fellow citizens and people who love peace all over the world. Martin Luther King was shot and killed this afternoon." The gathered crowd, unaware of the news, was devastated. When the cries from the crowd quieted down, he continued. In trying to dissuade the thousands from being overcome with anger and hate and retaliating with riots, he mentioned how his brother, John, was also shot by a white man and how he understood what they were feeling. In hundreds of cities across America that night riots broke out following the news of King's death, but not in Indianapolis, thanks to Robert Kennedy's words. It was probably his most memorable speech and it helped him secure the minority vote in Indianapolis.

After his speech, we went back to the Hotel Marriott and met with about two dozen black leaders. At first there was a lot of grumbling and subtle booing and angry murmuring when RFK tried to speak. Finally, a couple of scattered voices among the group said, "Quiet, Quiet, let him speak!" RFK began his talk about how his day had begun "First thing, I showered and got dressed. I had to catch a plane to come out here to the Midwest. As I began to leave, a couple of my children walked with me. They wanted me to go in the pool to swim with them. I told them how I was already late and that I had to get to the airport.

When I got on the plane there was a series of newspaper articles written, placed by brokers and business people, deploring the fact that I was too close to the minority community. Then, when I got to Indiana, the minority community accused me of not paying attention to their needs. Having this be my greeting was not very favorable or encouraging. I work for everyone, impartially. Some critics have been angry that I used too much of my energy for people like you, but I have to be fair and help groups like this who have special needs." Suddenly, RFK was politely interrupted by a dashiki clothed man. "Senator, that is fine talk." He then spread his arms like wings of a plane, gesticulating, "Senator, you will get on the big white plane and leave us only your words." RFK sternly responded to him, and put his hand on my arm and said, "I am leaving here, that's right, but my brother Ted's closest political friend is here, Gerry

Doherty. I am leaving him here in Indianapolis. If any of you have a problem, talk to him. That will be like talking to me."

RFK walked out of the room with me, waved his arms and thanked the gathering. As we walked down the hotel corridor toward the adjoining crosswalk, he produced a big cigar from his vest pocket. He stopped, lit it and took a puff. He blew out some smoke and, smiling, said, "Well, Gerry, I have most definitely assured your stay in Indianapolis to be an interesting one." We adjourned to his hotel room. It was filled with all sorts of people who had accompanied him to Indiana. It was like a Cecil B. DeMille movie set, a half dozen young women, bearded scholars and several speech writers.

RFK left the next day for Washington. About this time, Ted and Steve Smith had arrived in Indiana. Together, with Michael Riley, we planned our activities for the next couple of days. About noon, just as we finished our meeting, a well-dressed fellow came into the office. He was looking for some bumper stickers and half-a-dozen lawn signs. He was very sure of himself and asked a couple of questions about the campaign; he said he would be back in an hour to pick up the materials. As he left, he handed me a check with no dollar amount written, but it was signed. I pointed it out to him, and he rather cleverly said, "So fill it out!" Frankly, we were a little uneasy about his self-assured manner. We thought he might be a reporter from The Indianapolis Star, owned by Eugene Pulliam, who in the short time of Bob's campaign was gathering suggestions and ideas for a negative treatment campaign.

About five minutes after he left, Riley's secretary came in with a message for Riley. I asked her if she saw the man who had just left. She said "Yes! He looks familiar but I don't know his name." Her response raised further suspicion that he might be a plant, a reporter, perhaps. About five minutes later the sec-retary returned holding what appeared to be a *Time Magazine*. She said with a grin, "I knew I saw him somewhere, and here he is." A photo of the fellow, posed with a half-dozen other young men, was on the cover. They were cited as young leaders who were portrayed as up-and-coming young business stars. His name was Art Decio, owner of Skyline Homes in Elkhart, and his company was described as a growing success in the mo-bile home business. About an hour later, he came in to pick up his material. As he began to leave, I asked him what amount we should put on the check. He said, "You fill out the amount." He hurriedly left with his signs and posters. After he had gone, Steve Smith and I quizzically brainstormed the amount. Five thousand…ten thousand…before deciding to fill it out for twenty-five thousand dollars. Over time, Decio became enor-mously helpful in raising money for Robert Kennedy.

Around this time, I contacted my longtime friend Kevin Kelly in Charlestown, a former Marine who became very active in my first successful campaigns after leaving the service. He loved politics. His family of four brothers had been longtime supporters of mine. We all had gone to St. Mary's Grammar School in Charlestown. His mother was always one of my most helpful and well-liked workers in my very tough campaigns in Charlestown. After a campaign victory, everyone would be happy except for Kevin, who became subdued because there was no more work for him to do. He would rather campaign than eat. He was a great organizer, tireless worker and amaz-ingly resourceful. When I talked to him and explained what I was doing, he said, "Do you need any help?" He came the fol-lowing Tuesday to Indianapolis and stayed until we won in May. He was relentless, tireless and effective, and people liked working with him. He and I broke up the state into the eleven congressional districts. He developed target areas such as college districts, ethnic complexes, population events and minority centers. We assigned resources to our target areas based on which ones were most important. At the end of the second week, we had recruited some experienced political workers from Massachusetts, and as they arrived they were hustled off to their newly assigned congressional areas.

Over the second and third week we assigned very experienced Massachusetts coordinators to all eleven congressional districts. For example, to the Seventh District, the site of University of Indiana–Bloomington, went Pat Loftus from South Boston who had extensive and effective experience working for Congressman Joseph Moakley of South Boston. To the Third District went Hank Keohane, former Harvard football captain who had just returned from Africa after a two-year stint as an organizer for an academic group. Included in his area was South Bend, including Notre Dame and Fort Wayne. A longtime friend of mine, Carl Johnson, a state representative from Braintree, went into the Kokomo area. He was a former fireman and he stayed at the local firehouse until he got settled. Boston City Councilor Pat McDonough oversaw the area of central Indiana. Longtime friend and organizer Don Dowd, from West Springfield, worked down in the Evansville area. Grace Ann Barry, who led a group of Chicagoans, took over the First Congressional area, which included Gary and Hammond. Kevin Leary, a law associate of mine, headed the greater Muncie area. Frank Quirk, a former top assistant of Congressman Joseph Moakley, handled the two congressional districts in Indianapolis. Also joining our contingent was former Mayor of Fitchburg, Carlton Blackwell. John Douglas, from Chicago, was the son of former Senator Paul Douglas, a longtime friend of RFK. When RFK recruited him to come out to Indiana, he agreed to do so only if he could work with me, not over me. I was very happy with his efforts and delighted to work with him. I would always refer to him as the "goodwill campaign ambassador without portfolio." He was very successful in getting the various groups from New York to support me in our effort. It should be noted that all of those mentioned got housing at the YMCA, local colleges and private homes. Each one received no money except ten dollars a day for food.

In addition to this bevy of volunteers, we quickly established a communication nerve center in Indianapolis headquarters. It consisted of a center, staffed by three women, mimicking the "boiler room" from Ted's senatorial campaign, with each overseeing three or four congressional districts. Each member of the trio was in constant contact with their appropriate congressional coordinator. Toby Cohen, who worked as a coordinator in Ted's first campaign in 1961, joined our nerve center staff. Another was Maryellen Lyons, who had worked for the Democratic State Committee in Massachusetts. Her sister, Nancy, also helped with scheduling. Katie Murphy, a school teacher from Boston who took a furlough from her teaching position to help our effort in Indiana, was the third member of the contact center staff.

These women closely monitored their areas every day. Each read the local newspapers and were in contact with the various local organizations. There was a constant ebb and flow of information. This was coupled with the planning of local visits, based on information received from the contact center. Each day at four o'clock, I would sit with the three women and get an accurate assessment about what was going on in their respective areas. All this information was used as a bedrock for RFK's schedule. It also provided him with instant information about the various area or support people RFK would need. The system was not perfect, but it was a very helpful guide to gathering information about people, places and things.

Out of State Volunteers: Conflicts

Around mid-April, there were some bumps and bruises in our efforts. Shortly after most of the Massachusetts volunteers were in place, there was some friction between Ted's people from Massachusetts and Robert Kennedy's staff from New York. I was stretched out, putting the right people in the right places. I got an irate call from RFK's longtime and experienced advance man, Jerry Bruno. He started to screech at me over the phone. There was no one to pick him up at the airport and take him downtown to our headquarters. It was the second or third temper tantrum from RFK's New York staff workers. Finally, I said to him, "If you are as good as you think you are, you can find your way from the airport and if you can't, we don't need you!" Then I hung up. He stormed into town and screeched to everyone who would listen to him, "That Doherty is a fresh SOB!" Smith responded, "Gerry is a busy guy and he doesn't run a taxi service. He doesn't have time to hold hands for anxious people."

After the third week in Indiana, RFK's staff from New York started arriving in droves, with little knowledge about how things were organized. They began to question what provisions had been made for them and where they would be staying. In about the beginning of the third week, the RFK staff sent

Bobby into Lake County with little preparation. He rode with Lake County Treasurer, Lou Karras, who advised RFK to drop out. According to Karras, Bobby was going to lose badly to Governor Branigin in the primary. When RFK returned late that night, he summoned me, complaining that everybody around me were dopes and amateurs in the eyes of Karras. Just an hour before RFK returned to Indianapolis, one of our workers briefed me about the local democratic organization's all-out effort to defeat RFK. He handed me a very negative advertisement of RFK that was signed by no other than Lou Karras. I showed RFK the ad and said, "Is this the same Lou Karras who you said was advising you as a *friend* to drop out of the race?" He was stunned and became speechless. He was embarrassed and apologized.

Around that time, groups of students from various states – Illinois, Kentucky, Michigan and Ohio – began to show up. A young woman named BJ Warren popped up at our headquarters in Indianapolis. She had some experience organizing teams of volunteers for the peace movement. In a matter of days, she orchestrated several contingents of students and dispatched them to various target areas and populous cities. We housed them in the cellar of our headquarters, which was in the basement of a large, vacant theater. We slept three hundred students on mattresses provided by the campaign. That, coupled with forty appointed monitors, enabled the entire student effort to run smoothly. Regional captains deployed their young people whenever our local campaign effort needed foot soldiers.

Motivational Psychology Professor Surprise

Probably my most interesting learning experience throughout the Indiana campaign was a fortuitous session with a motivational psychology professor. The Friday before our second to last weekend effort, he came to our downtown headquarters and pleaded with our receptionist to see me. Because he was persistent, I agreed to see him. He told me he was going to monitor one of the canvassing groups the following day. He wanted to pose different questions and ideas for the diverse body of volunteers to use for contacting local voters. He wanted my support, which he got. The organizer of the group that he went out with gave me a phone number where I could contact him, and off they went.

Early Saturday morning our youthful militia fanned out to what we considered our key areas. We were concentrating on low- and middle-class working families in areas that had supported George Wallace in the Democratic Presidential Primary four years earlier. Furthermore, there were good-size, middle-class enclaves of Polish, German, Czech, Mexican, French and other ethnic groups spread throughout the state. There was also a cross-section of people who had come up from the south to work in the automobile plants. On weekends, our teams were dispatched to these various locales. The professor joined a group at a low-income area where George Wallace did well.

Late that Saturday afternoon and early evening our student pollsters began to return. At seven o'clock, I was just finishing a planning meeting when the motivational psychology professor appeared and pleaded again with my gatekeeper to see me. My assistant came in and told me of his request. I was interested in what he had found out in the field. When he came in, he was bubbling over with enthusiasm and information. In a sort of low-key manner, I asked how his day went. He excitedly said, "Great! We found it!" Puzzled, I said, "What did you find?" He said, "I was out with a group of energetic and motivated young people. We tried out every approach. Different questions, new ideas, various styles." Rather impatiently, I asked him, "What did you find?" He said, "The right approach, the right tactic!" "What was that?" I asked. "One of the student workers came up with the right key." I impatiently again said, "What did he do?" He explained how a student at one house was greeted by a man in work clothes, who asked him what he wanted. The young man said, "I am here to tell you about Robert Kennedy. His motto is to give people a hand-up rather than a hand-out." That was the students' message. The man in the doorway smiled and said, "That's what I want!"

The professor, noticing the positive response this slogan evoked, instructed the rest of our workers to use the same approach: "Would you vote for Robert Kennedy to give people a hand-up rather than a hand-out?" Universally, the slogan elicited a positive reaction. I was pleased with this explanation, and we began to use that query technique in all the sections that were low- to middle-income working areas. We developed a thoughtful plan of action to attract the various ethnic groups to support RFK. We also stimulated memories of John F. Kennedy and attracted the older group of votes by espousing Medicare, Medicaid, and other senior citizen issues. It was a way to organize the lower-middle income families.

Campaign Takes Shape

Late that same afternoon, I became aware of a meeting going on with Robert Kennedy and all the New Yorkers who had come to Indiana to help in the campaign. I was infuriated that this group was meeting privately with the candidate without me. I thought that I was purposely excluded. I brooded and thought maybe I should just go home. Shortly after the private session concluded, I bumped into David Burke, Ted's top aide. Furiously, I ranted about meetings held behind my back. Burke sternly responded, "Do you know anything about the gathering?" But before I could reply, he forcefully said, "It was about you! RFK said 'This is a tough campaign. Gerry Doherty, Ted's man, is in charge. If some of you don't like it then go back to New York. Do what Gerry tells you to do because I think he knows what he is doing. Understand? Let's all get back to work.'" Smiling, David said, "That's it!"

Already I was receiving help from members of Bob Kennedy's staff. His chief writers Adam Walinsky and Jeff Greenberg had been very supportive. They started to come to me for background information about various coordinators and workers. Larry O'Brien, who had resigned from the LBJ cabinet, came several times to Indiana to help on special projects. One of his key suggestions was to create phone banks, and that was extraordinarily successful. He recruited Matt Reese, who was very helpful in 1960 for JFK, to set up and oversee the phone calling network. He played a very important role in our phone operations. The phone bank effort quickly developed an unbelievable corps of unfound volunteers who then went door-to-door for RFK in most of the major cities. The operation intensified and multiplied our foot soldiers. It seemed we had Kennedy workers everywhere.

After a broad and meaningful plan was outlined, it was agreed that we had to give RFK more exposure in the ten or twelve major cities. There was a general feeling that RFK was another political outsider without a great sense of belonging in Indiana. We decided that he had to embark on an ambitious tour of the appropriate population centers. Some thought our agenda for action was fuzzy. Sheepishly, most of us agreed. We then decided that our congressional district coordinators should utilize their network of volunteers to determine the best way to accomplish our goal in their districts. Our major concern was to get the candidate to the field. Let people see Kennedy; feel him; touch him. Get him to mix and mingle with people in the crowds. His up-close magnetism might convert those who were unsure about him. It was simple. Get him out to more people so they could see him and hear him. Our regional coordinators across the state had the best sense of how to get crowds to see Kennedy, so each coordinator developed a game plan in their area; visits, speeches, rallies, and stops at local newspapers, radio and TV stations. Most importantly, let Hoosiers brush shoulders with the candidate.

Over the next three weeks, Kennedy crisscrossed Indiana. He made stops in nearly twenty large- and medium-sized cities and towns. His numerous local appearances, rallies and visits began to transform his image from the remote, outside politician into someone who the people could relate to, someone they could trust and believe. We were sensitive to their problems and needs. Gradually, he raised their pride. He was not distant. He was warm and friendly and liked the crowds – and they began to like him. A plan for more appearances began to emerge. Kennedy made trips into various sections of Indiana to visit homes and areas that encompassed Hoosier pride. Kennedy visited the home of Walt Whitman, the grave of Nancy Hanks Lincoln, President Lincoln's mother, and made time to visit the St. Francis Xavier Cathedral in Vincennes, Indiana.

To reinforce his appreciation of Indiana pride and history, he was scheduled on a trip through central Indiana. He made a colorful railroad trip on the old Wabash Cannonball train through Wabash, Huntington and Fort Wayne. Local officials rode with him on the trips. The pageantry saluted the old Hoosier pride. It was a live car train, with fiddlers entertaining the crowd. Every town turned out. Over and over, as the train went by, people sang the Wabash Cannonball Song. In every town where they stopped, large crowds cheered and saluted RFK. In Huntington, a crowd of more than three thousand people gathered. A young woman presented him with a petunia plant, which he promised to plant in the White House Garden when elected. He preached about education and its rising costs, which he would address when he was elected.

Gradually, the crowds began to intensify. His reception became more friendly and animated. Our local volunteer groups grew. On the nights he returned to Indianapolis, I would meet with him and we would talk about the day, its highs and its lows. Scheduling took advantage of the excitement and enthusiasm. His confidence began to build. Momentum began to swell. Almost everywhere our workers voluntarily went the extra mile for Bobby. The extensive telephone network of volunteers produced a new set of supporters. The consensus of our eleven congressional coordinators was upbeat. The growing crowds adopted him as one of their own. He had transformed into a

Hoosier. He was one of them. The excitement for RFK was ramping up and got so great that well-wishers even pulled him out of his car at one rally. He loved it and they loved him.

The Kennedy campaign continued to build momentum. His aides set up a system that sent out daily messages on radio. The public could also get the latest information when they contacted Kennedy headquarters. Notwithstanding the latest campaign swelling support, Eugene Pulliam, publisher of the *Indianapolis Star* and *Indianapolis News*, continued to block our coverage of Kennedy's efforts. RFK's name never appeared in their papers, except when his mother complained that his hair was too long. The newspapers covered every bit of Branigin's campaign. The only other time I can recall Robert Kennedy's name in the newspaper was when Gordon St. Angelo, Indiana Democratic State Chairman, publicly criticized RFK for buying the election. Nevertheless, despite the lack of help from the newspapers, we trudged on with the campaign.

Toward the end of the campaign on May sixth, RFK toured Gary with Mayor Richard Hatcher, the first black mayor, and Tony Zale, a Gary native and famous boxer. It was a symbolic effort to bring together two celebrities and highlight their united support. There had been in the last weeks of the campaign an effort to close the gap between white ethnics and African Americans. One could sense their merging of Kennedy support.

As part of the last drive to persuade voters, the Kennedy family, headed by Rose and Joan Kennedy, campaigned across Indiana. Prince Radziwill, who was married to Jacqueline Kennedy's sister, joined the family's last minute campaign effort and spoke of his opposition to the Russians in Poland. It was a fantastic and successful boost to the campaign.

Every bit of energy was in play for Kennedy by his field support groups, who created a feeling for Kennedy through appearances and campaign materials, developing a favorable thrust for his candidacy. The appeal to give people a hand-up rather than a hand-out seemed inspiring. His series of speeches and personal stance on issues developed interest. It was reflected by the growing crowds. At first people were skeptical to see another Kennedy, but invariably the gatherings expressed a more positive feeling about him. He was believable. He worked tirelessly, and gradually more of the crowds felt they could relate to him. He was being recognized. He became their champion.

Our campaign began receiving a very positive reaction to his appearances in various parts of the state. Blacks, low-middle income whites, Hispanics and other identifiable ethnic groups showed their enthusiasm and support. At headquarters, we could feel a sense of our new found supportive groups. Now we had to get Bob's supporters to the polls.

A determined thrust was underway to get election lists to contact voters and get them to the polls. These lists, unlike in Massachusetts, were not public records. However, many staff members in local election offices secretly made the voter rolls available to local Kennedy volunteers.

The opposition of the State Democratic Party, with their fully-backed support of Governor Branigin, turned out to be an advantage for us. They stayed out of our and way we stayed out of theirs. We had no bickering about who was in charge and no petty rivalries to overcome.

A subtle rivalry began to emerge between experienced Massachusetts political workers and RFK's senatorial staff from Washington. The fast-paced formation of a disciplined campaign created pressure, and certain tensions began to emerge. Sometimes RFK would anxiously say to Ted, "Does Gerry know what he is doing?" I remember that I would get a call from Ted who would say, "I hope you know what you are doing, Gerry?" He would explain that Robert felt I was really Ted's guy.

The telephone efforts to enlist and excite volunteers was a backstop in all the major cities and towns. The last weekend before the election, this army of recruited workers – all wearing their large campaign buttons – went to work. As we visited the neighborhoods over the weekend, we were like a swarm of bees buzzing from house to house, from street to street. This program was carried out in most of the major cities and towns. These workers also distributed an RFK tabloid, which stressed his goals when he became President. The activity of this swarm of workers also produced new people to help on Election Day.

In the closing days of the campaign, new but experienced recruits began to show up. There was a group of political workers who had been ostracized in Indiana, but they knew all the campaign tricks. I was contacted by a lawyer, Owen Mullen, who had been active politically for years. I checked with Michael Riley about him and he said that he was a knowledgeable outcast who knew all the angles of the political game. Michael Riley said I should meet him. Late one afternoon a week before the election, I met with him in a bar on the edge of downtown. I had with me Frank Quirk, from South Boston, who was our overall key person for Indianapolis. We got to the bar about twenty minutes before four, went in and were directed to a table in the back. We were greeted and introduced by himself: "I am Owen Mullen, a lawyer and a political junkie and am an outcast from Governor Branigin." He was a very self-assured lawyer.

He invited us to sit down. We gave him our names and involvement with Kennedy. He sarcastically said, "I know who you are and all I want is Kennedy to beat Branigin and all his flunky boys." We sat down. His well-tailored jacket was hanging on the back of the chair. He was nattily groomed in shirt sleeves. He had in front of himself two drinks, which later Frank Quirk identified as boilermakers. He asked if he could order drinks for us. I responded, "Yes, Coca-Cola." Frank said, "I'll have the same." Mullen quickly smiled, stood up and deviously extending his rolled-up shirt sleeved arms, "Coca-Cola? Would you boys like to dance?" We smiled. He sat down and snarled. "I know you are the right people to talk to about Kennedy," Owen said seriously. "Election Day here is loaded with potholes for newcomers." I quickly but seriously said, "Go ahead." He eagerly responded, "Do you know about the fast precincts and slow precincts?" I was puzzled and said, "No. Tell me and Frank what we should know."

He began, "Election Day starts with the polls opening at 6:30 a.m. That is earlier than most of the polling places around the country. This is or is supposed to be a concession to suit the farmers." I rudely interrupted him and said, "So?" He responded, somewhat angrily. "I'll tell you. There is illegitimate polling. Usually he or she who is in charge at the polling places is in the pocket of the ruling party. Here, the Democratic Party. In a district, say there are a thousand voters registered there. In these fast precincts, there are visually few voters around, but by 7:30 a.m., five hundred votes have already been cast. Voting officials are experienced and cute; they know which voters show up and which ones do not. And since there are very few witnesses around, they jiggle the machines, counting the votes of absent voters who they know will not actually show up. The votes are rigged for the election of the warden's favorite candidate. Here, that's Branigin."

Owen continued and said, "Then there are slow precincts. Usually in the minority districts of the cities. The candidate who wants to slow down the respective polling places has at their disposal a small army of people dressed in police uniforms. As the voters line up to vote, these impostors are equipped with flashbulb cameras. They take pictures of the voters waiting in line, causing voters to become uncomfortable, afraid of being photographed by imitation policemen. This process frightens many of the minority crowd in line and they disappear, greatly reducing the number of votes cast in the precincts." That was Mullen's briefing about electoral behavior, which he suggests will be performed by the governor's people.

Victory Shared with Bob and Ethel

On Election Day, reports of our activity became more assured. Apparently, our opponent's efforts were almost non-existent. At 7:05 p.m., the media announced that Kennedy had a clear victory over Branigin. Kennedy received 42 percent of the vote, with nearly eight hundred thousand votes. Branigin received 31 percent, and Eugene McCarthy received 27 percent. Surprisingly, only in upper-income Catholic areas Robert Kennedy did not do well.

The local television stations wanted Robert Kennedy to appear at their studio. His aide tracked me down and said I had to go with Kennedy, at his request, for an interview. I told his aide that I had to wait until our mostly Massachusetts workers could come back to Indianapolis. Some of them needed money, some of them needed a place to sleep, and others had transportation problems getting back to Massachusetts.

My wait for all of them to arrive stretched to nine o'clock that night. With our workers finally all back in Indianapolis, I told Bob's assistant that I could accompany him right away. I met Bob and his wife Ethel, and we went to the studio. We were told we had to wait about a half hour before we could be interviewed. After a hug from Ethel and a robust handshake from Bob, we sat down in the reception area of the studio. As we were seated, he leaned over and shook my hand again, and said softly, "Gerry you are Ted's good friend. You have been great in this fight for me and I hope now I can be considered your friend, like Ted?" I was moved to silence with gratitude. Then almost instantly the interviewer came out and ushered us into the studio. It was a great night. We both said it in different ways. Then we all went to celebrate. Ethel said happily, "We are like the Three Musketeers." The next morning our contingent of exhausted and jubilant workers took off for Boston. Altogether there were sixty-two happy warriors.

Robert F. Kennedy Assassination

The next day after our return, Bob and I got together. He asked if I could go out to California and help the effort there. I said I would like to, but I had to get home to catch up on my law business. However, I did agree to go to New York in early June, after the California fight was over.

The night of the California Primary, my wife Marilyn and I were watching the jubilation of Bob's victory on the television. My bags were packed for me to leave the next morning to go to New York and run Bob's efforts there. The news of his assassination flashed on the television. My wife and I were stunned. We said a prayer for him. Reality was stunning.

The day after Robert Kennedy's assassination in California, I went to New York to the chosen site for his funeral – St. Patrick's Cathedral. Bob Doherty, who had lived in New York for a long time, had reserved for my use a large hotel suite in downtown. There I set up an operation center for RFK's network of field workers, which I had scattered across the country as campaigners. They came from a host of states: Indiana, California, Washington, New York, New Jersey, Missouri and others. With the assistance of a group of volunteers, I was able to get them transportation from these places to New York. Ultimately, we housed over twenty-five RFK campaigners in the suite lent to me by Bob Doherty, and they slept on the floor.

Early the day before the funeral Mass, a massive problem arose. Attendance at the funeral required tickets. Late in the afternoon I discovered that tickets were restricted. A fellow from Ted's office was in charge. I went to him but he would only give me two tickets for admission to the services. After my pleading for additional tickets, he adamantly rebuffed me. We argued but to no avail. However, I recognized in his office an old friend from Boston, Nancy Lyons. On leaving the RFK office I nodded to her. Moments later, I called her from a payphone in the building lobby. I quickly told her my problem and asked if she could help. She said she would meet me at a restaurant next door in five minutes. She had a shopping bag, which she slyly deposited under the table. She softly said, "There is a box of tickets in the bag," then quickly left.

In her package, there were about a hundred tickets that I was able to distribute to all of our volunteers. Throughout the day, I had numerous requests and was able to accommodate all of the needs of our RFK corps from across the country. They all attended the Mass, even my old friend and tailor, Harry Chin. He was sitting so close to the front that people thought he was the Chinese Ambassador. The RFK corps' attendance at the funeral was a sad reward for all their campaign efforts. Robert Kennedy would have wanted them there. Many of them joined the RFK burial caravan on the train from New York to Washington for his burial at Arlington National Cemetery. Robert Kennedy would have been pleased with their commitment and their allegiance to their fallen leader.

Ted Calls to Reaffirm His Support

After Robert Kennedy's death, Ted took it very hard. He and a few of his close friends embarked on a several-week-long sailing trip off the coast of Maine. In the meantime, there was a meeting at the Sidney Hill Country Club to choose the Massachusetts delegates to be sent to the Democratic National Convention, which would be held in Chicago at the end of August. Due to the circumstances, there was a prevailing sense that Ted Kennedy should not and would not attend the convention. I suggested that the vice chairman of the delegation might have to lead the group of delegates instead. Bob Quinn, who was the Speaker of the Massachusetts House of Representatives, offered to lead the delegation and step in as acting chairman. I told Quinn that I would not nominate him, but that I would second him. However, Lester Hyman, Chairman of the State Committee, believed that he deserved to lead the delegation in Chicago.

At the gathering, I did as I promised and I seconded Bob Quinn. Some of Ted's staff were confused and befuddled. Hyman was surprised and contested the election as an alternate candidate for Chairman of the Massachusetts Delegates. Yet, Bob won overwhelmingly. The newspapers carried the story that Lester had Teddy's support and that my disloyalty to Ted was abominable. The papers berated and crucified me, calling me a traitor. It was suggested that I betrayed Ted and his choice of Hyman to ingratiate myself by giving Speaker Quinn the nomination because he would favor me as a lobbyist. They really battered me.

The ensuing days were upsetting around my house. My wife Marilyn was constantly in tears. After about five days of hearing of my treachery, disloyalty and betrayal of Ted, I received a phone call. Ted had docked his boat off the upper coast of Maine to pick up some supplies. He picked up several newspapers and saw the stories berating my support of Speaker Quinn. He called me on the phone one morning while I was having breakfast. "Gerry, you have been one of my best and most helpful friends over the years and you have never betrayed me. Don't listen to these news stories. You chose to support a longtime friend of yours in Speaker Quinn. Don't worry, I will straighten things out with my staff." Teddy called the newspapers, voicing his support of my decision to nominate Speaker Quinn, and altogether the berating stopped. We all now turned our attention to the upcoming Presidential election.

Gerard F. Doherty

Former Senator Ben Smith, Senators Ted Kennedy and Robert Kennedy - 1966.

David Burke, former Ted Kennedy aide and CBS News President, his wife Trixie and Gerard Doherty - 2006.

President Jimmy Carter's mother, Lillian Carter and Gerard Doherty.

Robert Kennedy accepting victory in the Indiana Democratic Primary with Ethel Kennedy and Gerard Doherty - 1968.

Ethel Kennedy and Gerard Doherty at the Kennedy Library - 2007.

Senator Ted Kennedy, Gerard Doherty and President Lyndon Johnson – 1964.

Jimmy Walsh, Dave Powers, former Assistant to President Kennedy, Billy Sutton and Gerard Doherty, all from Charlestown, MA.

Gerard Doherty with President Jimmy Carter - 1977.

Thank You Dinner with President Jimmy Carter - 1977.

The funeral of Pope John Paul I at the Vatican, Gerard Doherty, Frank Bellotti and President Carter's Mother among the American delegation – 1978.

Congressman Joe Moakley, Nancy Korman, Senator Kennedy, Congressman Jim Shannon, Dave Davis, Director of Mass Port Authority – 1980.

Boston Mayor Tom Menino and Angela Menino

Senator Kennedy paying tribute to Gerard Doherty on his 80th birthday.

State Senator Tom Birmingham, State Senate President William Bulger, Senator Ted Kennedy, Marilyn Doherty, Congressman Joseph and Beth Kennedy.

State Senator Joseph Timilty, Senate President William Bulger, President, Holyoke Community College David Bartley – 1996.

Robert Fitzgerald, Senator Kennedy and Gerard Doherty - 1980.

Admirals' Hill in Chelsea, MA was the site of the Chelsea Naval Hospital; its many buildings have been converted into more than 1000 residential units.

Marilyn and Gerard Doherty with Mayor Tom Menino.

William Swanson, CEO Raytheon, Caroline Kennedy, Gerard Doherty at Kennedy Library - 2004.

Former State Senator James and Margery Hennigan and Gerard Doherty - 2004.

Richard Donahue, former Counsel to President Kennedy and son and Gerard Doherty - 2004.

Former State Attorney General Bob Quinn and Father Quinn with Gerard Doherty - 1996.

Marilyn and Gerard Doherty with Vicky and Ted Kennedy - 2006.

Conan O'Brien and Gerard Doherty Kennedy Library Dinner - 2010.

Gerard Doherty and JFK Library Foundation Chairman Kenneth Feinberg.

Edward Doherty, Gerard Doherty, Senator Kennedy, Nancy Korman, Robert Fitzgerald - 1996.

Congressman Joseph Kennedy III and Gerard Doherty at Irish International Immigration Center breakfast meeting - 2014.

City of Boston Corporation Counsel, Eugene O'Flaherty, Gerry Doherty and Senator Edward Markey.

Gerard Doherty and Ted Kennedy at Kennedy Library annual Dinner - 2000.

Marilyn and Gerard Doherty at Kennedy Library annual Dinner - 2008.

Chapter 5

Jimmy Carter for President

In June of 1975, I supported Ted Kennedy's brother-in-law, Sargent Shriver, for President. Also running was Washington Senator Henry "Scoop" Jackson, who was an early favorite. However, in the fall, my friend Jim Hennigan supported Jimmy Carter as did State Senator Joe Timilty. Carter's people went to New York in June to plan for the Democratic National Convention. There were a lot of misgivings about Carter's strength in industrial states, like New York, Illinois, Ohio, Massachusetts, New Jersey, California and Pennsylvania that bothered many people. Adam Walinsky, former press secretary for Robert Kennedy, and others met with Carter advisors in New York. There was a lot of anxiety about Carter's appeal in such states. It was suggested that Carter bring in some experienced political organizers.

Joe Timilty was close to Carter's top advisors and he agreed with their opinion to bring in more experienced campaigners. He convinced Hamilton Jordan and Jody Powell to explore and come up with some names and ideas. Walinsky was very adamant about the need for experienced, veteran campaigners. He suggested my name among others. Timilty agreed and asked me to be interviewed. I was old and tired and reluctant to go. Now, I was very active in specialized, adaptive reuse of abandoned buildings for housing. I was adamant on not going. However, Ted eventually asked me to go down to New York and do it for him.

To satisfy Ted and Timilty, I went reluctantly for an interview. My mind was already made up. I did not want to get more actively involved in the Carter campaign. I told them I would help raise some money. I gave them some ideas as to what they should do. They liked the ideas and pleaded with me to get involved. I respectfully thanked them for singling me out for help, but declined the offer.

I went back to Boston and two weeks later they called and asked me to come to New York again and talk with the Carter people. They said, "You would be a great help in Jimmy Carter's effort." Timilty called the Carter people and made an appointment for me to meet again with Carter's staff. Jim King, who was a close aide to Ted Kennedy, encouraged me to at least respect Carter's acknowledgement and go to New York for another visit. Jim King was very close to the pollster Pat Caddell. Caddell was a volunteer in Ted's earlier campaigns as a freshman at Harvard. Over the years, Jim King became his mentor. Now, for short money, Caddell had become Carter's pollster. Over the years, Pat Caddell also became a good friend of mine. So, Jim King, Caddell and I all went to New York again for a meeting. At this point my interest and ego had begun to rise. I was intrigued with participating in a national campaign in a presidential election.

There were a lot of people there – Hamilton Jordan, Jim King, Jody Powell and Landon Butler. They pressed me very hard. It appealed to my ego. I then began to buckle. I played hard to get with some arrogance. I agreed to help, but only on my terms. I would go for a trial of two weeks, during which time I would only help if I received the approval of both Governor Hugh Carey and New York Mayor Abraham Beame. Beame's people had gotten calls by Kevin White not to use me, but they contacted me anyway. Then, I would make my own decision as to whether I stayed or not after the two weeks was up. I would not be paid. My travel would be covered by the campaign, but I would provide my own housing. Also, I would recognize Bill vanden Heuvel and Midge Costanza, who was a Democratic activist and a city councilor from Rochester, New York, as co-chairmen of the campaign. But, most of all, I would be in complete charge except for a reasonable overview by Hamilton Jordan. Everyone listened to my desires and readily agreed. The last admonition was that if either Mayor Beame or Governor Carey had problems with me, I would leave. Hamilton nodded his head, stood up and shook my hand, and said, "I will see you in two weeks at the Carter headquarters in downtown."

Campaign Manager in New York for Carter

From my work in adaptive reuse, I had a close contact with a New York lawyer, Steve Ross, with whom I worked in real estate syndication. He suggested to me that I live with him and get away from the hubbub of the campaign. I did so, and consequently lived about four doors down from Steve Smith, Teddy's brother-in-law, on East 63rd Street in the Upper East Side.

I started with the campaign in mid-August, and met on the first day with co-chairmen Midge Costanza and Bill vanden Heuvel, whom I knew from his involvement with the Kennedys. It was pleasant. I assured them that I respected their position and their loyalty to Jimmy Carter. After about an hour's session with them, I met with Carter's staff. I assured them that I had already learned of their good reputations and also assured them we would all get along fine. I stressed that I was there as an unpaid volunteer, as I had been with all my experiences with the Kennedys. Any success I had, had been due to the people like his staff. "All of you have been selected because of your hard work and effectiveness. It is my hope and expectation we can work together as an effective group that will result in Governor Carter's victory. I will enjoy working with all of you. My door will always be open. In the next several days I will meet with all of you individually. Lastly, Governor Carter will be here in New York the day after Labor Day. Our collective efforts are to make a success of his visit."

Filling 1,800 Seat Hall: Local Leaders No Help

Carter's headquarters had scheduled an appearance the day after Labor Day at the Brooklyn College auditorium, which held eighteen hundred seats. A lot of work had to be done to make a success of his appearance. On the third day of the New York campaign, I scheduled a meeting with Democratic Party leaders of the five boroughs of New York and the surrounding state Democratic Chairmen of Westchester, Nassau and Orange counties. It was held at our headquarters in downtown New York, and at around 11 a.m. I introduced myself. My talk was brief – a little biography about myself, with some emphasis on my experience with the Kennedys. When it was over I asked for questions. A hand went up just in front of me. I recognized the middle-aged man before me. I asked for his name and affiliation. The fellow standing in front of me responded, "Meade Esposito, Chairman of Brooklyn." After a brief background story about himself, he got to the purpose of his attendance at the meeting. "How do we get funds from you to run the Carter campaign in our districts?" I quickly responded that I didn't have any money to distribute at the moment. Esposito quickly commented, "In that case, I am busy and don't have the time for meetings like this. I have a lot of things to do. Good bye." There was a rustle of feet as the other attendees got up and left without any promise of their help for the Carter visit, six days away.

Now what was I to do? My first thought was to seek help from the many colleges in the city. However, very few of them were in session. My first task then was to visit the site in Brooklyn to get a better look at the eighteen hundred seat auditorium. After a quick visit to the hall, I was walking back to my car when I noticed, stopped at a red light, a yellow school bus with lettering on the side, "Second Baptist Church." I asked my assistant, Joan Gross, "How many Baptist churches are there in and around the city?" She looked puzzled and said, "I'm not sure, why?" I responded, "Well, Jimmy Carter is a Baptist. New York is heavily Catholic and Jewish. Why don't we try calling all the Baptist churches in and around the city and invite them to Carter's appearance." I figured that Carter would like to appear before a friendly crowd. It was a dippy idea but it could work. We came to learn that in the city and surrounding areas there were dozens of Baptist Churches.

Over the next few days, Joan got some fellow volunteers to make calls to all the Baptist churches in and around the city. Our callers informed them that Jimmy Carter was coming in a few days. Our callers received a very enthusiastic and positive response. In the meantime, calls were made to all the democratic clubs, local legislators, and city officials inviting them to Carter's appearance. They were pleased because our callers emphasized that Carter respected their long-term loyalty to the Democratic Party.

On Labor Day, we visited the hall in Brooklyn and made sure all the appropriate arrangements were in place. We all hoped with some luck that the Carter event would be at least satisfactory. In the few days I was at headquarters, Joan helped me with getting the names of city and state officials I should get to know. She was very efficient and remarkably resourceful at compiling the various lists of legislators and other important people I should come to know.

On Tuesday, the day of the event, I got up early at six o'clock and drove, accompanied by Joan Gross, to the site of Carter's appearance. The parking lot was almost empty. I assured myself that it was early and went to a nearby coffee shop with Joan. I had pins and needles similar to what I experienced before playing high school football. We strolled back to the college at about eight o'clock. There were patches of yellow school buses scattered about the large parking area and lined up at the entrance was a long line of yellow vehicles. As we approached, the tide of yellow expanded before our eyes. As we got closer we could readily identify their origin. Almost everyone in Metropolitan New York was represented along with a flood of assorted New York church buses. At eight thirty, the lot was filled with church vehicles and a smattering of passenger cars. We entered the hall. Political dignitaries were already crowding on the stage. By nine o'clock there was limited standing room in the side aisles.

Carter came into the hall to a thunderous reception. Our group's efforts had been extremely successful. Carter was delighted by the reception. On his way off the stage he shook my hand and thanked me, then he was gone. The overwhelming show of support for Carter was a great send off for the formal opening of his campaign in New York. Our collective efforts were recognized by Carter and the entire campaign staff. His well-received appearance established that the New York Carter campaign organization was not only credible, but also effectively competent. It transformed a lot of my critical doubters, who were at first skeptical of me and my role as chief of Carter's New York campaign, into believers.

After Carter's appearance in Brooklyn, my self-induced probation of two weeks had expired. Interestingly, a couple of Mayor Beame's personal assistants told me again that Mayor Kevin White from Boston called the mayor criticizing me, saying that I wasn't a good guy and that my only interest resided with the Kennedys. However, Mayor Beame did not give Kevin White's criticism any credence.

Governor Hugh Carey's Chief of Staff, David Burke, was an old friend of mine and formerly had been Ted Kennedy's Chief of Staff for several years. His wife, Trixie, was wonderful to me when we tried to nominate Frank Morrissey for a Federal Judgeship. David was terrific in Carter's campaign in New York. He knew the state and had contact with all the active and effective people both in politics and business. After my arrival in New York, he suggested that I meet the Secretary of State, Mario Cuomo. Cuomo's position was appointive. Governor Carey had selected him to represent the Governor as an ombudsman. In his capacity, Mario had access to New York State airplane to utilize in his various and sundry duties around the state. We became very good friends. In his multitude of duties, he knew of the political hotspots. He volunteered to help me and accompany me on visits to events around New York. He was a marvelous help, ally, and most of all a good friend. New York was a big state to manage and he made my political introductions to almost everyone seem easy.

There were varied political areas of New York. We organized a successful effort to reach the target areas quickly. First, we had to divide the state into the city as the center and the rest of the state. The city was split into the respective five boroughs – the Bronx, Brooklyn, Manhattan, Queens and Staten Island. The remainder of the state was separated into different areas of concentration focusing on a cluster of cities based on their individuality and importance – Buffalo, Rochester, Syracuse and Greater Long Island. In New York City, itself, policies, people and politics were separate organizationally from the rest of the state. Besides the twenty-some odd Democratic members of Congress, the two-principal people who were around were Governor Carey and Mayor Beame. One thing I perceived early, with the size of the state and scattered political locales, was that information about everything and everyone happening in the state had to be known immediately and communicated to the appropriate people. Significant information, any information about the Presidential campaign, had to be communicated immediately. Information awareness and its dissemination had to be completed simultaneously to all the campaign districts, especially any important matter involving a district.

Kennedy Game Plan Put to Work for Carter

After a lot of thought and wondering how to do it, I came up with the same scheme we used for both Ted and Robert Kennedy. My solution was to acquire trusted, smart, and energetic women, especially any with affiliation to the governor or the mayor. These women would sit together with me in my office, where they would witness the arrival of information. They were with me when any kind of news came to me. It was their responsibility to select what effect it would have upon their constituency, state or city and communicate the relevant matters to the proper parties in those districts. Congressman Ed Koch played the role of coordinator. His work as the coordinator was a key part of Carter's victory. He worked hard and possessed credibility with all the other Democratic leaders. He had a contact person in his office who would distribute information as quickly as possible. This operation worked well.

In every campaign I managed, I always organized a room of telephone callers. I usually found a friend – or the friend of a friend in states outside of Massachusetts – who would loan his office in the evening for the purpose of making telephone calls on behalf of my candidate. After acquiring the space, the next step was to locate a list of registered voters that contained accurate telephone numbers. I usually found these through Democratic Party officials. To recruit callers, I'd ask a young person to gather friends to make the calls and I would supply the beer and pizza.

The script for the calls was always the same: "I am (name) calling on behalf of (name of candidate) to remind you of the (date) election, and I want to remind you to vote." This positive message demonstrated that my candidate was providing a service, and the simple message maximized the number of voters we could contact. To engage in a conversation about the issues would bog down the callers and alienate some voters. This tactic also worked well for Jimmy Carter.

In the meantime, I had to develop a relationship with the various key political figures and business groups around the state. Time and time again, David Burke gave me the right name for whatever need I had. David Burke and Governor Carey set up a memorable dinner for me at an Italian restaurant. Altogether there were about fourteen people there. Important representatives of labor parties attended, including Paul Smith of the Seafarer Union who was Chairman of the AFL-CIO. Appropriately, David sat me next to Paul Smith at this dinner. For the first twenty minutes of the meal, I had already gotten to know most of the attendees. Burke told me great things about Paul Smith. This did not evoke any kind of response towards me from Smith. Finally, very subtly, I said to Paul Smith, "I was very friendly with the Longshoremen Union 799 in Charlestown." Smith, for the first time, remarked, "Oh!" I then said, "When I was a legislator, I was very close to them at their union. Perhaps you might have known my cousin, Dan Doherty, their business agent." Paul became very animated. "Do I know him?" he said, "He saved my life!" It seemed that the whole table, including the governor, snapped to attention. David Burke said, "How, Paul?" Paul took a sip of water and said, "I was at an unofficial meeting with half a dozen waterfront union guys. It got loud and rough and a good-sized guy grabbed me by my throat. A voice shouted, 'Leave him alone!' The person responded, 'You try and make me.' And in a flash, Dan Doherty jumped up, hit the guy and knocked him off his feet. I was stunned. The battered fellow was laying there on the floor. It was like a movie scene. Dan came over to me and asked if I was all right after things settled down." Paul and I got along well from there on out.

The next day Paul called me and asked what he could do to be helpful. I told him that whatever he could do would be much appreciated. He immediately sent over to the headquarters checks made out to the campaign. He also gave me a couple of contacts at the joint unions' office in case I needed more money or foot soldiers. Throughout the campaign, he was tremendous and a treasured friend. Most importantly, Paul helped my credibility with the unions who at the outset were troubled by my Harvard background. Some called me and said they would like to help me because Paul told them I was a regular guy.

Back at the control room, the state was broken up into four regional centers. Each was assigned a contact person. Every afternoon at four o'clock I would review with each of the women the day's activities. They reviewed their designated area and each reported any significant happening in their area and newspaper coverage of all aspects of Carter's efforts, both regionally and locally. Any political activity was closely followed and reported. Our campaign in New York was rolling along well.

In my early days running Carter's New York campaign, I imposed strict control. One of my requirements was that we had a series of staff meetings first thing in the morning. About midway through the campaign we had our regular staff meetings at nine in the morning. On a Tuesday morning session, just after we started this trend of staff meetings, Judy our press person came in about ten minutes late. She was very apologetic. Someone volunteered that the traffic was the cause of her tardiness. She replied, "No. I had a problem with my diaphragm." I said,

"Oh, I know how you feel, some mornings I have a problem with mine." There was silence, then laughter filled the room. She apologetically said, "Not that diaphragm." Everyone laughed. I did not. Later Judy's difficulty was explained to me. Rather sheepishly, I grimaced and understood her difficulty. However, our campaign continued to speed along. Everything and everyone was getting along well. We were all in sync.

One of my constant challenges throughout the campaign was the various important political leaders who kept badgering me for money for special campaign activity. I would always listen to their pleas and then I would pull out my leather reminder book from my vest pocket and deliberately point to my planner, saying, "The money you're looking for just doesn't fit into our master plan. And this comes straight from Washington headquarters, so they will not allow it." Amazingly, their pleading would not end until election eve. Little did they know, my leather reminder book just outlined daily activities while also serving as a collector of dinner receipts and other forgotten cards and pieces of paper.

The control center and I would capsulize the information, activities, candidates and Republican activity. I would compile all the material and articles about Carter's representatives in the state. It was giving me a very timely overview and I would use it to recommend future activity for Carter. Around the beginning of October, we had a good road map for our overall campaign approach. With about a month to go, we had an accurate sense of how and where we should focus our major efforts. We caucused with various groups to keep them informed about local trends, issues and events. The Carter central office was for the most part very responsive. However, with about two weeks to go, a problem developed. Our gathering of information gave us necessary and appropriate agendas for Carter's upcoming trips. Queens County was a major target. We thought that Carter had to make an appearance. I called the central scheduling center with my proposed places where Carter needed exposure. About an hour later a woman called who was the coordinator of campaign trips. She said she had vetoed Carter's going to our target area. We argued. She became very angry and said to me that I had everything all "F#@#$% Up!" I retorted, "Well, since you are the one running everything, fine. But I had an agreement with Carter that I was in charge, not just in name, so tell Hamilton Jordan to get someone to take my place. I will be on the plane back to Boston at one o'clock." I hung up.

About a half hour later, Hamilton Jordan called and stated there was some misunderstanding. "Carter will go wherever you want, Gerry." About ten days later Carter toured Queens and had two very successful events. That evening, Carter stayed overnight in New York and he sent word for me to see him at his hotel. I got there at about nine o'clock. He had a couple of aides at the entry to his suite who checked me out then I was escorted into Jimmy Carter's bedroom. He and his wife, Rosalynn, greeted me. He said his campaign day was very successful and well organized, and his reception was exceptional. He then said, "Gerry, I don't know what you did or how you did it, but everything is going along well here. Before you came here there was constant bickering and fighting of various groups, and I don't know how you have stopped that. There were always several fights and disagreements. Now no one is complaining and our efforts are going smoothly. Keep it up! If you need me call Hamilton and I will get back to you immediately."

Father Greeley and the Catholic Vote

Reports from across the state were encouraging. Both Mayor Beame's aides and Governor Carey sensed Carter was making progress. Personally, frictions were minimized. However, there were other important external aspects and factors that had to be accommodated. When I arrived in New York in late August, I noted that the New York Post printed a weekly column written by Father Andrew Greeley of Chicago. It was not very positive towards Jimmy Carter. I got in touch with Grace Ann Barry in Chicago, who was very helpful in Robert Kennedy's Indiana effort. She was very friendly with Father Greeley. I asked if she could set up a meeting for me with him. A day after our conversation, she phoned and said she scheduled for us to meet the following week. We met over breakfast in downtown New York. I discreetly talked about his weekly column and his treatment of Jimmy Carter. He noted that Carter had very few if any Catholics in his group of top advisors. We discussed the matter pleasantly. He asked me if I could name any other Catholics, other than myself, with whom he was friendly. I temporized. I really didn't know. However, we ultimately concluded our meeting pleasantly.

After that session, I called Grace Ann Barry and thanked her and asked if she could talk to Father Greeley on my behalf. A couple of weeks later, his column's tone seemed to soften. His articles suggested that neither Ford nor Carter were probably worth supporting. Finally, just before Election Day, Father Greeley subtly praised Carter, saying he found Carter more supportive and favorable because he espoused many of the social programs that Greeley supported. All things being equal, Carter was more of a humanitarian choice. Around this time, Bishop

Mugavero of Brooklyn surprised us when he recited his feelings of support for Carter because of ten social issues that were important to the Bishop. Carter's position was the same on nine of the ten. The only difference was the issue of abortion, on which they disagreed.

Ford to City: "Drop Dead"

Later in October, I bumped into David Garth who was friendly with Governor Carey and particularly friendly with my very good friend David Burke, the former Chief of Staff for Ted Kennedy. As Election Day came closer, I continued to talk with Garth about what I should be doing. He was somewhat helpful with a couple of ideas and suggestions. Then, with nearly two weeks to go until the election, New York City was on the verge of bankruptcy. Both civic and political leaders implored President Ford for help. At their insistence, President Ford came to New York with his political and financial advisors. They had several information gathering sessions, and he seemed to be supportive. However, a few days after his fact-finding mission in New York, he announced that it was financially unfeasible to honor the city's request for help, asserting that he would refuse to support such a bailout. The next day, the New York Daily News depicted a cartoon of President Ford on the front page with the caption, "Ford to City: Drop Dead." Not only was the city disappointed and discouraged, everyone was angry at his arrogant refusal.

Early that day, David Garth called me unexpectedly. He said he had an idea. First, he asked me if I've ever been to Grand Central Station or Penn Station at eight o'clock in the morning.

I said, "No." He said, "You go to both places tomorrow morning." I said, "Why?" He angrily said, "Just go!" So, the following early morning I went to both stations and saw massive crowds of commuters streaming through the train stations. I returned to my office and called him and rather quizzically reported my finding to him. I said, "What does that have to do with me and the election?" Garth responded, "These commuters come from all the communities surrounding the city. Their jobs are in the city. If the city goes down financially these jobs are in question. So, their jobs are in jeopardy. City failure would drastically affect them. Now you can get these commuters involved. Revamp the Post cartoon with Ford telling the city to 'Drop Dead.' They will get the message and vote against him."

I met in an hour with an artist and we redid the New York Post cartoon. We made a few changes and ordered five thousand two-by-four sized posters to paste up around the city. We did the same on palm cards and got volunteers to distribute them to commuters. The new revamped cartoon illustrated Ford in a toga and an olive branch around his head, posing with his thumb pointed downward. Over his head was the cut out from the New York Daily News, with the caption "Drop Dead." All this was done in about two hours, and then delivery of the materials started. Quickly the cards were given out. However, people either refused them or dropped them. One of our assistant campaigners recognized the problem. Passengers thought they were being given small discount cards for massage parlors, which was the current practice early in the morning in downtown New York. We quickly rectified the situation and gave out new longer and narrower cards of Ford's picture. People recognized the message and said they would show Ford what they thought of him.

After the second day of distribution, I got a call from the editor of the Daily News. He was an old acquaintance of mine from New Bedford. He said we would have to stop the use of his cartoon. If we did not, we would be forced to do so. He said his lawyer was away but he would get in touch with me if we did not stop. Nevertheless, the damage was done; we could feel the surge from the commuters. Enthusiasm for Carter was genuinely heartfelt.

With about five days to go until the election, I recruited a group of Massachusetts legislators to come and help in New York. I wanted them to monitor the major democratic cities and check on the Carter campaign's activity. Senator Jim McIntyre of Quincy went to Niagara and Buffalo to oversee their operations. Bob Quinn, a former Attorney General of Massachusetts, sent some others to Syracuse, Rochester and Albany. They seemed to work out okay.

We then ran into a few missteps due to poor communication with Carter's schedulers. One error was the campaign's failure to have Carter attend the Alfred Smith Dinner a week before the election. I was stunned. I learned that the dinner was a must after Harry Truman attended the bipartisan banquet in 1948. Both candidates had attended that function the week before the final election for President. The function was sponsored by largely Catholic groups to honor the memory of former New York Governor Alfred E. Smith, who had been a former candidate for President. It was a must on all political calendars. There was a slip-up on scheduling and the invitation was totally lost by Carter's scheduling office in Washington. The error could not be rectified despite input from all the democratic leaders in New York. The damage was done.

The Hasidic Vote in Brooklyn

Back in 1948. Truman started another important tradition, visiting the Hasidic Chief Rabbi in Williamsburg, Brooklyn. In that portion of Brooklyn there were thousands of Hasidic Jews. Every four years, the democratic nominee for President made the visit to pay his respects to the Chief Rabbi. It was always around the time of the Alfred E. Smith Dinner. It became a catastrophic problem. Carter's headquarters had dropped the ball again and had accepted another engagement in another critical state to shore up his vote. The heat from his absence became tremendous. I and all the Democratic leaders in New York were angry and embarrassed. The stupidity of the mix-up created unbelievable criticism. Catholics felt insulted and now Carter's failure to visit the Williamsburg community angered the Jewish population.

Throughout the campaign, I formed a great relationship with Rabbi Reuben who was a Hasidic and worked for Mayor Beame. His work was centered on the Hasidic community. He was very upset about the uproar and the campaign stupidity. Before this turmoil, he had arranged for me to visit Williamsburg and meet with the Satmar Rabbis and congregations. In Williamsburg, there were several different sects. Each had come from different parts of Eastern Europe.

A week before Carter's failure to attend, I had a meeting with the Satmar. Lois Cohen, a social worker who worked with Hasidic communities for the City of New York scheduled a visit with them, which I was to attend. The visit was scheduled for seven o'clock. She was to meet me at six o'clock and drive to Brooklyn. She was late. I was nervous and when she arrived fifteen minutes late, I really scolded her, "What happened?" She explained her problem. She said, "Look at me! I had to find a dress with long sleeves to wear and that took some time. Also, if you haven't noticed, I am flat chested today, I had to bind up my chest to look modest. That's why I was late!"

We rushed to Williamsburg and made good time. When we got there, we were looking for the building where we were to meet with the Satmar group. We became confused about the address. At about that time, there was a steady stream of men dressed in black, all wearing hats. I said to Lois, "Ask them where the building is." She said, "I can't! I will bet they won't talk to me." She got out of the car and approached them. They completely ignored her. I got out of the car and asked some other men where I was to go and they pointed out where the meeting was located. I started to go and asked Lois to hurry. She said tersely, "I can't go. They will not let me into the meeting." I rather pensively said, "Okay" and went alone into the building and walked up a short flight of stairs into a good-sized meeting room. There were twenty men sitting there. Their dress was all identical, black hat with a round border, black frock coat, black knickers and white stockings. They all had beards. A man who was their leader got up and greeted me. I outlined why I was there on behalf of Governor Carter. We talked about everything, particularly about their schools in Williamsburg. They had over five thousand students enrolled in their system.

As he described his system, it seemed very similar to the Catholic school system, which I knew well. Many of the processes were similar to the Charlestown parochial school system. They also were adamantly opposed to birth control. Except for their beards and dress it was reminiscent of old Charlestown. Our meeting was fascinating. I thanked them and we parted very cordially. We met with all the different groups in the Hasidic community, and they were a great help to Jimmy Carter.

When I got back to Lois in the car it was almost an hour and a half later. I was very bubbly and happily excited. Finally, Lois turned to me and said, "They are all thugs." I was surprised at her angry tone and then she snarled, "Did they tell you about women? And how women are banished to the second-floor galleries during their religious services? And did they tell you how their women have to wear wigs in public?" I was startled but knew enough to quietly go back to the campaign office. Lois left me off in downtown and said she was going to rearrange her disguised bosom. Foolishly, upon her leaving, I said, "Lois, we are bosom friends!" She groaned and drove off.

Election Eve at Gracie Mansion

On election eve, Mayor Beame organized a meeting at Gracie Mansion that was the official residence of the Mayor of New York. In attendance were all the Democratic borough leaders from New York City, the State Party Chairman, Patrick Cunningham, myself and some of my staff. The purpose of the meeting was to review Election Day plans and inspire the leaders to a great effort on Election Day. The highlight of the meeting was a telephone call on a speaker phone from Jimmy Carter, who thanked everyone and reminded them that the work does not end until the polls are closed. The Mayor opened the meeting with a greeting to all and a message promoting getting the vote out. I talked about thanking them and offered my own reminder about working hard on Election Day.

Then there were renewed calls to me for "street money" on Election Day. Several offered statements that Rockefeller had one million dollars in cash on the streets of New York on Election Day. As much as I said there was no money for this, the leaders became louder in their protest. When it was announced Jimmy Carter was on the phone, the talk ceased and there was respectful silence. After the call, the State Chairman summed up the meeting by urging everyone to work hard on Election Day and then he turned to me and added – "Doherty, I expect you and the other "boiled dinners" you brought from Boston to be on a plane the day after the election back to Boston." Those in attendance seconded that thought. The meeting ended on a happy note.

Election Day and Victory

Early on Election Day, the polls were open at 6:30 a.m. Election Day activity throbbed. Everyone in the campaign seemed to be active and energetic. Across the state, Election Day plans and preparation were pulsating. Rabbi Reuben called me not long after the polls opened; we had a problem. He was very alarmed that in the Hasidic areas of Brooklyn, already about three thousand votes had been cast and they were all for Ford. It was incredibly disastrous for Carter.

Alarmed and anxious, I asked, "Why?" He angrily retorted, "Carter disrespected the Hasidic Chief Rabbi when he did not visit him the day of the Alfred E. Smith Dinner. When his failure to attend was discovered, the Rabbi got even more upset. Reuben said the early vote was all for Ford. I decided to call the mayor. It was almost seven o'clock before I reached his assistant. Mayor Beame knew we had a problem. Together we worked out a plan to get Carter's vote up in the Hasidic community. He had already started action. He had assembled his best staff people to call around and recruit all the rabbis in the area. They were raising a whole army of Hasidic rabbis. Sound trucks with loud speakers were being dispatched to the streets of Williamsburg to get the community out to vote for Carter. Mayor Beame went into the Williamsburg area just before eight o'clock and personally used all the rabbis and elders to promote Carter in this election. He personally talked to all the various rabbis and local leaders. From eight o'clock on it seemed that all the votes being cast were for Carter. The Williamsburg area had seventeen thousand Hasidic votes. When the polls closed, Carter received fourteen thousand and Ford had three thousand votes. As the night went on, Carter's vote with Ford continued neck and neck.

Historically in the Presidential Election, New York, New Jersey and Connecticut voted the same. Anxiety for Carter became alarming when the polls in Connecticut had closed at seven o'clock and Ford had carried it. Then, Ford won New Jersey. Uncertainty and doubt began to dishearten the Carter headquarters. At about 10 p.m. a New York radio station reported Ford the winner. Jitters swelled. Tension was everywhere.

Just around that time, one of my aides pointed out that the votes from the Bronx had not yet been tallied. We quickly checked some of our people in the Bronx who had access to scattered precinct votes. Carter had done very well. Even though they were scattered it seemed to give credence to the fact that Carter's performance in the area was well-received. I asked one of my assistants to check the election department of the city for the Bronx vote. He said that the Bronx vote was still out and then my thoughts focused on what might be happening. I called David Burke, who was Governor Carey's chief advisor, and asked him to talk to the Governor and ask him to talk to the leader of the Bronx Democrats, Patrick Cunningham, who was also Chairman of the State Democratic Party. Five minutes later David called to tell me that Governor had talked to Cunningham and I was right. He was up to something. It turned out that Cunningham was holding onto to the votes until it seemed as though Carter would lose New York, and then he was going to come out with the votes to make it seem as if he was the hero, with all eyes on him riding over the horizon delivering Carter the election.

I called Pat Caddell who was with Carter and told him what was going on. Still the winner was in doubt. Finally, at 1:30 a.m. the vote was final. Carter had carried the State of New York. About an hour later as we were closing, Jimmy Carter called to thank our group. He was put on speaker phone, and everyone cheered his message. I then went home to bed.

The next day I cleared out my office and returned home to Charlestown.

Meeting a Polish Cardinal in St. Patrick's Cathedral

While I was in New York I would go to St. Patrick's Cathedral on Fifth Avenue for Sunday Mass. One Sunday it was announced that there was a visiting Cardinal, Cardinal Wojtyla from Krakow, Poland and that he would receive visitors after the Mass. I joined the line of people to meet the Cardinal. When we met, I told him I was a friend of Ted Buczko from Salem,

Massachusetts. Cardinal Wojtyla told me he knew him well and said he was a good friend, and that he had said Mass in Ted Buczko's parish in Salem a couple of times.

I served in the legislature with Ted Buczko. In 1964, Ted Kennedy was able to get him appointed postmaster for Salem, and after the death of the State Auditor, Thomas J. Buckley, Ted Kennedy and I recommended that he be appointed to fill that position. He was the State Auditor until 1980 when he was appointed a judge by Governor Ed King.

Good Relations with the Carter White House

Harold Basser, the president of Taylor, Woodrow and Blitman and a partner of mine on several construction projects, asked me to arrange a meeting in Washington with a high government official to discuss American housing policy for Sir Frank Taylor, chairman and founder of the Taylor Woodrow companies.

Sir Frank Taylor started building houses in 1934 when he was 16 years old, and throughout his career his companies built hundreds of thousands of homes worldwide. The company grew to be one of the largest construction companies in the world, expanding its capabilities to include nuclear plants, new harbors and infrastructure projects.

I called some of my friends in the Carter White House who I had met in the campaign and they arranged a White House meeting place. I accompanied Sir Frank Taylor, Harold Basser and Jack Curry, a young Taylor executive, to the White House. To my surprise and delight, we were shown to a small meeting room next door to the Oval Office. Meeting with us were White House and HUD officials responsible for housing policy. It was a very good meeting and Sir Frank Taylor and Harold Basser were very thankful to me for arranging it.

On the way out of the White House, Jack Curry questioned me on my repeated absences from the meeting. He said, "How could you leave an important meeting in the White House so many times?" I didn't want to explain but Jack was very persistent. I told him my absences were caused by my meeting with Jimmy Carter's staff, who wanted me to come to the White House to work as counsel to President Carter. Each time I declined the offer and went back to the housing meeting, they would recall me to offer more reasons why I should take the job. Jack's curiosity was satisfied. I declined as I was very rooted to my home in Charlestown and Boston.

My Friend Mayor Koch

That was not to be the end of questions from Jack Curry, whom I came to admire. Jack was often asking me questions about different events and people. I did not always have a good answer for him so I would say, "You never know who you may run into in the restroom." When Jack got that answer, he knew no more information was coming.

I began to rely on Jack for assessing housing opportunities, so I sent him to meet with Mayor Ed Koch of New York City. I met Ed Koch through the Carter campaign and we became good friends. When he was elected mayor, I called him to congratulate him and during our conversation he asked me to send a representative to see him about housing opportunities the City of New York had available for private developers.

Jack went to New York and met with the mayor at an office in the headquarters of the Department of Public Works, where the mayor met with people he did not want exposed to the press. Jack reviewed the opportunities with the mayor and some of his staff.

Before Jack returned to Boston, Mayor Koch called me and said he had a good meeting with Jack, but asked that in the future I send someone who would not address him as "Mayor Coke."

When Jack came to my office upon his return, our conversation started with: "Jack," say "Mayor Koch as in Scotch." We repeated that exercise three more times.

Jack was embarrassed but no real harm was done.

Chapter 6

<u>Reconnecting with Civil Rights</u>

In March of 1977, President Jimmy Carter came to speak to a group in Clinton, Massachusetts. Before his public meeting, he had a private session with a group of Massachusetts Democratic leaders. Ted acted as his host. The gathering included Massachusetts Governor Michael S. Dukakis, U.S. Senator Paul Tsongas, Worcester Congressman Joe Early and Congressman Eddie Boland from Springfield. President Carter had asked me to join him. We had become friendly following his victory in New York in November. He also asked then State Senator Joseph F. Timilty to attend. Timilty had campaigned successfully for Mr. Carter in Pennsylvania. The session was a unique experience for me. It was President Carter's intention to keep in contact with political allies, not only in big cities but in smaller towns like that of Clinton, located in central Massachusetts. Keep in touch, as he said.

About three weeks later the President had organized a similar event in Memphis, to socialize with his election coordinators. One of his political allies attending the gathering was Aaron Henry, a newly elected Congressman and a pharmacist from Clarksdale, Mississippi. In 1972, Henry corresponded with Ted Kennedy for advice. Henry had organized a group of mostly minority residents to form the Mississippi Freedom Party, to fight for minority civil rights. In recent months, there had been a series of shootings and killings in Mississippi during civil rights protests. After much conversation, Senator Kennedy invited Aaron Henry for a face-to-face conference in Washington. Both recognized the serious nature of the challenge. They talked about how he and his brother, Robert Kennedy, had handled similar problems in their campaigns. Ted stared for a moment and then said he would ask a pair of his associates to help Henry in Mississippi.

Following the meeting with Henry, Ted contacted me along with one of his aides, Jim King, who was the senior member of the Kennedy's Boston office, to help in Henry's efforts. We flew to Memphis, Tennessee, and rented a car to drive to Henry's house. We were cautioned to rent a car with Mississippi license plates to avoid suspicion. It took us several hours to drive the rural, winding roads to Clarksdale. Aaron invited us to stay at his home because in Clarksdale there were no hotels. We arrived late in the afternoon. Early that evening there was a protest march condemning the mistreatment of minority students in the local schools. As the parade activities ended, it began to rain. We adjourned to Aaron's kitchen, where about twelve of us chatted over drinks and snacks. The rain became very heavy around nine o'clock. Suddenly, without warning, Aaron walked across the kitchen and shouted out his rear door into the rain, "I hope all you red neck bastards drown." Bewildered, I quizzically looked around and someone volunteered an explanation for Aaron's actions. Several months earlier, Aaron and his group hosted a similar protest march. Following that day's activities, late into the night, a few people attempted to blow up Henry's house. Aaron was concerned that they might try to do it again. But, luckily, the rain had probably thwarted that effort.

Around 11:00 p.m. Aaron showed us to the double-bedded room on the first floor, where we would be staying for the night. However, about every half hour either Jim King or I would ask the other, "Can you still hear the rain?" We both agreed that the pouring rain acted as our protection against another bombing. About seven the next morning, we were served grits for breakfast. For the remainder of the day, we attended different meetings with the Mississippi Freedom Party members. The rest of our trip was thankfully less exhilarating than our first night at Aaron Henry's house.

Aaron was subsequently elected to the Mississippi House of Representatives and proved to be an effective legislator. Many years later we had a reunion where he noted how helpful Jim King and I were in his political life.

Visit to the USSR for President Carter

About a month after Carter's post-election political tours around the country, I received a call from one of his staff members, Landon Butler, a contact person for me during the Carter campaign. President Carter had remembered that I spoke Russian. He had Landon call me to invite me to go to the Soviet Union on an information gathering visit to several major cities – Moscow, St. Petersburg, Kiev, and Vilnius, the capital of Lithuania. Accompanying me on this journey was an assortment of business leaders, five in all, from around the United States.

Our Russian itinerary included four days in each of the cities. Our routines were well established. We had breakfast at our hotel each morning at about eight o'clock. Then we would meet with local officials to discuss their plans and ideas for housing in their own communities. In the afternoon, we would visit recommended points of interest in each city. We engaged in question and answer discussions with residents and officials, some of whom were very intense during the sessions. In the evening, we would enter social discussion at dinner, which was then followed by entertainment, mostly musicals or some other theatrical productions.

Our meetings were run by the local board of planning and development whose top member was invariably a member of the Communist Party. However, in Kiev, the party director turned the meeting over to his chief architect who was a Ukrainian. This arrangement was followed in Lithuania, employing the same practice of using local people.

In Kiev, the Ukrainian architect discussed four projects for review. He displayed each of the developments and asked for our opinions after each presentation. The first two proposals were rather bland, we said. He responded by saying they were done by a special Russian team, which evoked polite applause. Then, in a lively manner, he displayed two more model development proposals. They appeared to us well designed. They were effusively praised. He said they were the works of a native designer. A week later in Lithuania, the same review was repeated. The plans of the Russian architect were politely applauded; the showing of the Lithuanian designs was enthusiastically applauded.

One memorable event occurred at the gathering of our group in a Kiev restaurant. There were about twenty of us gathered for dinner. The party included some wives of our hosts, the local architects. As I was talking with several spouses, the door to the room suddenly burst open. The guest with whom I was talking was startled by a woman screaming and laughing. Showing great emotion, she waved to him and shouted blissfully, "Sergey is in the university. He is in!" The room quieted down and she explained that Sergey, their son, had been accepted at the Academy College. I looked perplexed. Her husband beamed! I questioned, "If he had not been chosen for the academy what would have happened to him?" His father responded with a smile, "Our boy would have had to go into the army."

Our next visit was to Vilnius, Lithuania. Upon our arrival, we met with some builders and planners. On the second day we were in Vilnius, on an afternoon tour of the city, we came across a red brick structure that had a small entry from a small porch. We could see people entering the building. It was about five-fifteen. My curiosity prompted me to cross the street and open the door. I poked my head inside and saw to my amazement that it was a church, a Catholic church, filled. I turned to my colleagues and mentioned that there was a service going on. We all went in to rubber neck. Our team leader, a Russian woman shouted, "Nyet, Nyet!" Ignoring her shouting, I went in and the rest of my group joined me. It had started to rain. We gathered inside in the foyer quietly so as not to disturb the service in progress. Our leader opened the door behind us and screamed in English, "Out, Out!" Our group started out and as we left I put a handful of rubles in the collection box. My colleagues all did the same as our guide continued to scream, "Nyet, Nyet!" She was standing in the rain, soaked to her skin. Mockingly, I said to her, "If you had come into the church you would not have gotten soaked." She angrily put her finger into my face and screamed, "Nyet, Nyet!" and in Russian called me an idiot.

One way I fought back against our guide was with my uncanny ability to tell time. Someone would ask "what time is it?" I would squint, look at the sun and respond with the correct time. Finally, the guide confronted me and asked how can you tell time and you do not have a watch? I told her I would squint and look at the horizon and tell the correct time. She did not believe me and suspected I was playing a trick on her. One cloudy day I was discovered.

Our visit to Vilnius was the most interesting of our tours. It has an old town center dating back four centuries. It had a mellow feeling of old world character. Lithuania was generally very charming and its people very friendly. However, they did not like their Russian overseers. The standard joke was when a Russian asked for directions to their desired destination, the Lithuanian obligingly gave them directions to the local train station. Implicit was the message, "Get out of our town!" One of the oppressive acts of the controlling Russian authorities was to require all marriages to be civil. The ruling Communist authority forbade Catholic ceremonies. These weddings were countered later by the traditional Catholic matrimony. The people candidly talked about the fake Russian wedding and within days it was eclipsed by the standard Catholic sacrament of marriage.

After my own run-in with our Russian tour guide, she showed me her fangs. For the rest of our trip to Lithuania and back to St. Petersburg, she became a real witch. When we got back to our last stop, she became antagonistic towards me. For example, in St. Petersburg she would give me bogus directions.

I recall she would tell me that our group was to leave the hotel at seven in the morning. I would be there at that time except her instructions to everyone else would be for an hour later. In the evening, she would tell me to dress formally for a special dinner meeting when it was a very informal session. It was a couple of days of misdirection and confusion for me, but I survived.

On our last day, a Sunday, she turned us over to a local architect, Sergei Rappaport. He was about thirty-five, fluent in English and very helpful throughout the day. We went to a late afternoon concert, which we enjoyed. You could sense the feeling of friendship amongst our group. After the musical performance, Sergei invited us back to his apartment for tea and cake. He lived in an old, well-maintained apartment that was situated in a 1900 vintage building. His living quarters were made up of five rooms. He lived there with his wife and two children, but they were away in the country on his wife's official vacation. His mother and father also shared the apartment. His mother was an artifact restorer for various museums; his father was a school principal. We had a delightful evening with tea and tasty meringue biscuits. It was a pleasant interlude.

After about a two hour stay with Sergei and his mother and father, we returned relaxed and happy to our hotel. The next morning, we were ready to leave for the airport for our trip back to the United States. As I entered the lobby of the hotel, I noticed our guide from the Republic of Georgia was arguing with the ugly Russian guide. They were getting almost violent. She started to threaten him about his interference. She complained that Sergei should be reported because he broke the rules about entertaining foreign guests at his home. Finally, Sergei, in an angry tone chimed in and demanded, "How can you, as a Jew, report active Jews for their show of hospitality?" She was surprised and remained quiet. And it was disclosed that she was on the lowest rung of the ladder of guides. She was not a Communist Party member. She had limited security status and was still a junior operative at the age of thirty-five.

At the airport, we bid farewell to our two Russian development specialists. I turned to our Russian guide and thanked her. She smiled sheepishly. When I returned to Boston, I spent much of my time and energy working on my law practice. However, President Carter kept in contact with me personally on various occasions. For example, he invited Marilyn and me on multiple vacations to his Lake Lanier home in Georgia, which we had visited during the 1976 campaign. It was at Lake Lanier that we mapped out our strategy for the late fall campaign of that coming year.

President Carter's Delegation to Rome for Pope's Funeral

In the fall of 1978, Pope John Paul I unexpectedly died. A White House staff member called me, on Carter's behalf, saying that the President was assembling a delegation to attend the Pope's funeral. President Carter had asked that I be called and invited to the funeral as President Carter's "acting personal representative." Neither the President nor his wife could attend the funeral Mass of Pope John Paul I. I was honored at the request. The delegation consisted of Governor Ella Grasso of Connecticut, Mayor Edward Koch of New York, Massachusetts Attorney General Frank Bellotti, Senator Thomas Eagleton of Missouri, Governor Mario Cuomo of New York, and myself. Our group, together with Miss Lillian Carter, the President's mother, flew to Rome overnight in a special Air Force plane. Upon arrival, we were ushered quickly to the Excelsior Hotel for breakfast. After that we were escorted into one of the hotel ballrooms. Gathered there were two dozen tailors. They quickly measured us and fitted us appropriately in tailcoats, wing collared shirts, dark pants and tall black hats and guided us to appointed seats in Vatican Square for the afternoon funeral Mass. Interestingly, seating was based on when a country was founded. The Belgium delegation was seated in the front row. The United States delegation was seated about halfway back from the front. The funeral Mass lasted about two and a half hours. To protect us from the intermittent rain, young student clerics stood behind each of our chairs holding umbrellas. As I intently watched and closely followed the proceedings, the sun suddenly popped out; umbrellas were folded up. I intuitively looked up to the new found sunny skies and I thought of all my early school travails with my third and fourth grade teacher, Sister Edwardine at St Mary's in Charlestown, and instinctively smiled up to the heavens and thought to myself, "Sister Edwardine, I finally made it!"

After the Mass and its closing ceremonies, we were spirited to the Italian Embassy where Ambassador John Volpe entertained us and proffered a scrumptious dinner. At about nine o'clock, our much traveled and exhausted delegation was escorted back to the Excelsior Hotel and bedded down for the night.

Reconnecting with Cardinal Wojtyla

The next day we had an eleven o'clock appointment to call upon the College of Cardinals, including several from Massachusetts: Cardinal Law and Cardinal Wright. While at the College I encountered Cardinal Wojtyła; he remembered me and our conversation in New York about his good friend Ted Buczko. The next day, Cardinal Wojtyla became Pope John Paul II.

Ted Kennedy v. Jimmy Carter 1980

After a much enjoyed but short hiatus from formal politics, Tim Kraft, Carter's campaign manager, came to visit me in late August of 1979. After an exchange of pleasantries, he told me that President Carter had sent him to talk to me about the upcoming Presidential Election. He told me that Ted Kennedy was making a run for President in 1980. Tim somewhat sympathetically said, "The President has had a great relationship with you and is very appreciative of your helpful support. He also knows you are a very close friend of Ted Kennedy. However, he would like you to stay neutral in the upcoming campaign." I was surprised. Ted hadn't even hinted to me about his intention to run. Somewhat shocked by Tim's information, I said sadly, "President Carter has been a great friend. However, if Ted runs I would have to support him." Tim soberly said, "I figured that. I will let the President know." Our meeting concluded with both of us very uneasy. About a week later, Steven Smith called me and said that Ted was running and wanted me to help. I responded "Of course I will help him. What do you need me to do?" Steve Smith said, "You are a great friend. I will call you in a couple of days to talk about the next step."

Florida Caucus

In a subsequent phone call Steve Smith told me he was thinking about Ted challenging Jimmy Carter in the presidential primary. I told him I thought it would be a difficult run and that I wanted first to do some research about the first election, which was the Florida caucus in October. I always believed in assessing chances for victory before deciding to enter a political race.

I contacted my good friend Kevin Kelly, from Charlestown, and asked him to organize four or five friends who could go to Florida for about a week to assess Ted's chances on the ground. To finance the operation and to provide expenses for Kevin and his friends, I contacted the political action committee of a national union. The PAC provided the funds for the operatives, political data, and a list of democratic contacts in all parts of Florida. Kevin and friends were to identify themselves as representatives of the union's political action committee whose goal was to assess the strength of President Carter and other potential opponents in the upcoming Florida caucus.

Kevin and his group went to Orlando and from there fanned out across the state. Each was given the names and contact information for key democrats whom they would contact. After four days of travelling in the state and talking to political contacts, the group met in Daytona to trade notes and impressions. The universal conclusion: there was no substantial support for a Kennedy campaign. I informed Ted and Steve of this and they decided not to openly support the Draft Kennedy movement.

A day later, Steve phoned me again and asked me about Chicago and the people there. I told him I was friendly with young Bill Daley who was the son of former mayor of Chicago and political figurehead Richard Daley, but otherwise I had no experience in that city. Smith asked me to go the next day to Chicago and visit with their new mayor, Jane Byrne. He added that she, and almost every public official in Chicago, had already endorsed Carter for re-election. Two days later Steve Smith and I flew to Chicago and met with Mayor Byrne. She seemed ill at ease. She talked about JFK and her admiration for his family and her love for their commerce center, the Merchandise Mart, which was owned by the Kennedy family. Steve gave a recollection of the Kennedys in Chicago. Mayor Byrne admitted, with some embarrassment, her support of Carter after Steve chatted with her. She said, "Let me think about it and we will talk again later today." At our afternoon meeting she seemed almost ebullient. Just as soon as we sat down to face her, she said, "I love the Kennedys. Their presence at the Merchandise Mart has been wonderful. I'll change my position and support Ted."

Overnight, when her change of support for Ted became known, she was blasted by the newspapers. Carter supporters in Chicago lambasted her mercilessly. The former Democratic National Chairman, Bob Strauss, complained bitterly in the media. He criticized Mayor Byrne as a "chicken" and he said he will "make her into chicken salad before it was over."

A year earlier, the city suffered a very immobilizing series of snowstorms. The city was paralyzed for weeks. The chairman of the city council was acting mayor and seemed to be a shoo-in for election. Jane Byrne was a minor bureaucrat and was his only opposition. The acting mayor was savagely berated for his ineffectiveness and lack of leadership in the city during the snowstorms and the unknown bureaucrat, Jane Byrne, capitalized on the voters' anger and was elected mayor.

The Daleys were displeased with her handling of the upcoming election after she announced her early support of Carter, then switched her support to Ted Kennedy. By way of background, Chicago always had a great feeling of warmth and love for JFK. Steve Smith and I went to Chicago after Ted Kennedy announced his candidacy in mid-October. I stayed in Chicago and set up Kennedy's campaign structure. Around this time, Ted Kennedy had a terrible interview with Roger Mudd, in which he was unprepared to speak on the Chappaquiddick accident, and was unfocused and tongue-tied when asked why he wanted to become President. The interview was devastating for Ted in the polls.

Then in November, American hostages were taken in Iran by a group of Islamist students. Carter's approval ratings soared due to his calm and effective leadership during this stressful time. As a result, Ted's popularity in the polls caused him to lose thirty points in one week. He became the brunt of a political disaster. His loss of support in Illinois was horrendous. It was described as the unprecedented political collapse of his campaign. The confusion, anger and rejection paralyzed any opportunity for popular support in our effort on his behalf. Any hope we had of attracting volunteers for Ted's candidacy vanished. All the political leaders headed by the Daley family abandoned Ted's candidacy.

Our money from Washington dried up. Our campaign efforts were stymied. I worked hopelessly trying to stop the political hemorrhaging. The group that I headed for Kennedy was dispirited by the strong anti-Kennedy feeling. Yet, amazingly, despite our campaign efforts being thwarted, we continued to have a small and devoted group of volunteers who soldiered on. Ted made several visits to Illinois that were duds and his popularity ultimately leveled off at about 33 percent. Things were tough. For example, my wife Marilyn came out from Boston to help. She was a gallant advocate for Ted. Her speaking engagements were for the most part in Catholic high schools. At best, she was silently received. There was no applause. She could sense everywhere she went the displeasure of her audiences. Mercifully, there were only a few boos but there was very little applause.

Then in January, after Ted lost badly in Iowa, some of his paid workers came to Illinois. They were demanding, arrogant and badgered our few volunteers. At one point, I personally and physically threatened them for their overall behavior. Finally, Kennedy's disastrous campaign finished around the seventh of March. He lost by a margin of two to one. In all my years of politics and campaigns, my experience in Chicago was by far the most brutal. I must say that the only relieving factor was the wonderful and continued support we received from our very faithful volunteers. They were great. Throughout my various campaigns, over forty years, they were the most marvelous, hardworking and dedicated.

About the first of April, I was back to my law practice. It was busy. Despite my long absence, it bumped along thanks to my staff, headed by my assistant Elinore Shiels, my nephew, lawyer Ed Doherty, and my law associate Kevin Leary.

In late April, there was an organizational meeting to select about one third of our allotment of delegates to the National Convention. I was out of the country at the time, but I had many friends at the meeting including my longtime friend, former State Chairman David Harrison, and some other of my old allies who lobbied effectively for my candidacy. Despite my absence, they worked for me. I received one of the highest number of votes to be a delegate. An old and good friend in Senator Kennedy's office alerted my friends that some of the paid professional organizers plotted to defeat my selection as a delegate.

Sometime in May, in Worcester, there was the second session to choose the remaining two thirds of delegates. I was present that day and two different people, whom I hardly knew but had always been helpful to Ted Kennedy, approached me. They both told the same story of how the imported professional handlers were going to keep the two of them off the list of successful delegates. After hearing their stories, many of my old friends and I hindered the plot and these longtime, loyal supporters of Ted Kennedy were elected delegates.

In the meantime, Ted's campaign posted a series of wins in the large industrial states like New York and California, but these were not enough. Carter was renominated for President. The convention was held late in August. However, Ted seemed to have a new vitality and on the floor of the convention he made his much inspiring speech, "Sailing against the Wind," which he concluded in his crescendo voice: "The work goes on, the cause endures, the hope still lives, and the dream shall never die." The convention floor roared its approval with a seemingly endless demonstration. His reception was overwhelmingly enthusiastic.

Reuniting with Jimmy Carter

Two days after the convention, Ted called me at my office. He thanked me for my longtime efforts in Illinois. Then he said he had been called by President Carter who thanked him for his graciousness in his concession speech. He offered to raise money for Ted's campaign debt. The President also asked Ted if I would go back to New York and run his campaign there, as I did in 1976. Ted asked me if I would do that for him. Having run Carter's campaign four years earlier in New York, I said that it might be awkward for me because of broken promises. However, I would be willing to go someplace else. Later that week I had a conversation with Carter and we agreed that I would go to New Jersey. Early in September, after Labor Day, I traveled to New Jersey with Carter, where I stayed throughout the remainder of the campaign.

Carter introduced me to then Governor Brendan Byrne. Having been in politics for forty years, I met many outstanding leaders and figures. I must say Brendan Byrne was among the best I have ever had the good fortune of meeting. He was extraordinarily helpful in every way. I can only describe him as a truly superlative individual.

We opened the Carter campaign headquarters in Trenton, where we struggled for the duration of the campaign. Volunteers were hard to come by. Our location after dark was difficult to attract interested supporters. We kept our center of operations in Trenton, but we developed an energetic following in Princeton, which was about ten miles away. Princeton College generated some enthusiasm and enough supporters to enable us to raise some energetic activity.

The Governor was wonderfully supportive and enthusiastic, which constantly boosted my morale. Once or twice a week he would take me by helicopter to various parts of the state to campaign. He and his staff would arrange for me to meet and talk to assorted Democratic leaders, legislators and mayors. He was very helpful and created a positive sense of Carter across the state. Over the last four weeks we were able to generate some enthusiasm for Carter, which generated awareness for the campaign. Yet it wasn't enough. Reagan prevailed. After the election, I returned to Boston and busied myself with my law business.

Back to the Practice of Law

During the 1970s, I became very active in a few different redevelopment projects around Massachusetts. The first was across the river from Charlestown in the City of Chelsea. Acting at the direction of the Navy Department, the General Services Administration was determined to access some seventy acres of land in Chelsea, commonly and collectively known as the Chelsea Naval Hospital. The property consisted of eight buildings, including a commandant's house, four duplex captain's quarters, two large four-story buildings that formerly served as hospital facilities, a chapel and a recreational building. It fronted on the mouth of the Mystic River as it flowed into Boston Harbor. Despite its picturesque setting and development potential, efforts by GSA to sell the land and its scattering of buildings for more than a year were unsuccessful. Quite possibly because the land was within the boundaries of the City of Chelsea, and Chelsea was a downtrodden, financially burdened city, there was little interest. Both the Commonwealth of Massachusetts and Chelsea itself declined to become involved as purchasers.

In 1978, I was approached by a friend and client, Edward A. Fish, owner of Peabody Construction Co, Inc. of Braintree, who had become a developer and a general contractor. He asked me to join him in acquiring and developing the naval hospital site. With the assistance of some of my colleagues in the legislature, the City of Chelsea, its then Mayor Joel Pressman, and the City's Department of Communities and Development, headed by Michael Glavin, we composed a complex development agreement whereby the City of Chelsea would purchase the land for the lump sum of $3.6 million with a mortgage loan in the same amount from the Commonwealth's Government Land Bank. Mr. Fish and I initially formed a limited partnership under the name of Chelsea Hill Associates, and thereafter many sub entities with which we subdivided the land and acquired parcels for development. Upon the completion of development of each parcel, we paid the City of Chelsea, and it in turn repaid the Government Land Bank. Through mortgage financing provided by the Massachusetts Housing Finance Agency, and rental subsidies provided by the federal Department of Housing and Urban Development (HUD), we had developed one hundred sixty units of affordable housing for the elderly in one single building. Shortly thereafter, we interested a non-profit developer from Michigan to develop another one hundred units of affordable housing for the elderly through HUD. Very quickly, we had turned the abandoned site into a viable residential complex with two hundred sixty units in all.

As part of our development agreement with the City of Chelsea, we agreed to assume responsibility for the installation and maintenance of the roads, present and future, accessing and traversing the site. Additionally, we were required to assume responsibility for the maintenance of street lights, and more significantly, water service. The city had engaged a contractor to construct a pumping station to service the projected number of residential units on the site. Months into its contract, after many delays, the city called the developer in default. The water pressure thereafter failed and we then had a crisis on our hands. Fortunately, Ted Kennedy had been able to have HUD designate the City of Chelsea for an Urban Development Action Grant (UDAG), which we could use for the completion of the pumping station. Until the pumping station was complete, the top of the site was virtually without water. Ed Fish and I recalled that the Town of Falmouth had an antique water pumping engine, which was only shown off in ceremonies and parades. With our fingers crossed, we rented the pump from Falmouth, brought it to Chelsea and it served the interim purpose of providing adequate water pressure to the site.

As I mentioned, there were other buildings on the site that we needed to address. There was a granite building on what is now called Commandant's Way, along the water, built in 1835. It originally served as the Navy's first medical building and was put into service in 1836 as the first military hospital. Later, that same year, a brick structure situated near the top of the site was opened as an additional facility. It was in this building that John F. Kennedy recuperated from his war injuries in 1944. Both structures, with the assistance of preservation tax credits, were converted into housing units. The original commandant's house, located just north of the Tobin Bridge and overlooking the river, was acquired through us by an architectural firm called the Architectural Team, headed by Bob Verrier, and today serves as headquarters for more than sixty architects and draftsmen.

The completed multifaceted development consists of 791 units of rental and condominium housing. Happily, these units are full today and their respective tenants and owners seem to be very satisfied. Our work in the area was completed by 1990. Today, the overall development is known as Admiral's Hill.

The next development that occupied my time during and after my involvement in the 1976 and 1980 elections was situated in Peabody, Massachusetts. Around the early 1970s, I was active with a development team that focused on a large, abandoned processing plant. Our group consisted of two locals, Phil Singleton, an architect, and Larry Collier, a Lynn businessman. Our architect was Tim Anderson, a former Harvard football captain. This group included a joint venture with a British company, Taylor Woodrow, and our own active construction builder, Howard Blitman of New York. Together we formed an entity seeking to redevelop a network of the abandoned buildings formerly occupied by Swift Meat Packing into a six hundred unit housing complex for low- and middle-income residents.

The complicated process of approval had to go through the Peabody City Council. At the hearing for the approval, the large meeting room was crowded with several hundred people, many of whom were nostalgic about having worked in these buildings. The chairman of the city council was a Peabody mailman. Tim Anderson, our architect, was sort of a quirky fellow. Instead of using a briefcase to house his papers, Anderson used a mailman's bag to hold his plans and outlines for the hearing. It was looked upon as his good luck charm. The chairman was favorably impressed with Tim Anderson and his bag. He later told someone he thought our architect was a former mailman. As chairman of the meeting, he moved our session along and took a vote in favor of our proposal, at which point the gathered audience applauded.

Tim Anderson and our engineers worked feverishly to come up with an attractive plan. It was a successful night for our development group.

Our principals went to Chicago to finalize the purchase of the Peabody buildings for a million dollars. Our final dealings with the representatives of the Swift people were concluded at about one in the morning. The vice president of Swift seemed to be a bit uneasy. As we sat together, at the culmination of the purchase, he was apprehensive that we were biting off more than we could chew. I assured him that we were comfortable going forward with the purchase.

HUD was somewhat uncertain about bringing so many units on to the market at once. Therefore, they limited our activity to two phases. The first phase was limited to four hundred units. Only after this first complex was fully occupied, would they allow us to go forward with the second development phase, nearly three years later. These additional two hundred units were quickly completed and, all together, our proposal for the six hundred units was achieved. I was involved in a multitude of other development projects in and around Greater Boston throughout my years after formal politics, but Admiral's Hill and Peabody took up most of my time.

Busing and Charlestown

After I became State Chairman in December 1962, Ted made an effort to take me around and introduced me to some of President Kennedy's close contemporaries. One of them was W. Arthur Garrity, a newly appointed Federal United States Attorney. He was a key supporter for the President during his campaign in the Midwest, particularly in Wisconsin. Ted would arrange several luncheons over the years with Arthur Garrity and me, for the most part to discuss job placements for lawyers who had been helpful to the President. In 1963, President Kennedy appointed Arthur Garrity a Federal District Court Judge. Occasionally I would see him at charitable and educational dinners, and we would politely exchange greetings. Over time we maintained a level of remoteness in our greetings, following his busing decision. It was instigated by me.

Fast forward to 1972. Judge Garrity was selected randomly to take on the task of solving segregation in the Boston Public School system. After a troublesome and contentious legal journey, Judge Garrity established forced desegregation of public schools by busing students to surrounding neighborhoods to attend school. Throughout most of the city, there was an upheaval of demonstration, picketing and a community-wide display of anger. South Boston and Charlestown were especially belligerent and violently opposed Judge Garrity's plan. These areas exploded with charged resistance.

Some of my immediate neighbors on my street in Charlestown were catatonic. Violent demonstrations erupted everywhere. Riot police were ever present. Helicopters buzzed over our raucous streets. All day long our neighborhood was patrolled by police officers wielding their batons. This display of subjugation continued for weeks.

Several times a week, from 1974 to 1975, three or four hundred women in Charlestown would gather in front of St. Catherine's Church, at the bottom of Bunker Hill Street, at ten in the morning, and then walk up the hill about a quarter mile to St. Francis's Church. Along the way, they recited the rosary and sang religious songs, praying that busing would stop and that peace and quiet would return to our town. Their efforts were to no avail. Throughout the years of forced busing, flocks of families with school-aged children moved to the busing-free surrounding suburbs. This migration created empty homes, scattered around Charlestown. The wholesale flight of families left a blight of abandonment. The remaining population was made up of people who could not afford to move, or families who could afford to put their children in private or parochial schools. Charlestown's population was halved in a few years. Only the large public housing population stayed intact.

Gradually, the vacant houses slowly began to be filled by young couples with preschool-aged children – a trend that continued into the eighties. Whimsically, these new residents were labeled as "Toonies" as compared to longtime residents who were called "Townies." Our way of life was totally changed by the busing commands.

The Charlestown community had become hostile towards Ted Kennedy and Congressman Tip O'Neill for their outspoken support of busing in Boston. Both lost to their opponents in the primaries for their re-election. Privately, I had conducted a poll to forecast their chances in their respective, final elections. My poll predictions showed overwhelming victories for both Ted and Tip O'Neill in their final elections, which was a very close depiction of how the actual elections panned out. Both men were re-elected to their offices, yet not without a prevailing sense of hostility from residents throughout the City of Boston.

Ted and I disagreed about the decision of Judge Arthur Garrity that brought busing to Boston and tore apart my home district of Charlestown. He never tried to persuade me to change my mind, nor did I try to change his mind. We both expressed our views on the topic and it never interfered with our relationship.

One day, as the case was heading to the United States Supreme Court, Ted called me and said he heard that the busing opponents were having difficulty raising money for the printing of their brief for the Court. The brief would require some unusual and expensive printing of maps. He told me to let the anti-busing lawyers know that their printing bill would be taken care of, but that his involvement was not to be made public. I asked Ted why he was doing it and he said that he wanted the court argument to be fair for both sides, and if one side did not have full and complete legal briefs it would not be fair.

Sometime in March of 1981, I received a call from an author who had just completed a book that chronicled the events surrounding forced busing in Boston public schools, focusing on its effects on three different Boston families. He wanted to meet with some Charlestown residents to get their reactions and opinions about Federal Judge Arthur Garrity's decision to bus students to other neighborhoods in Boston as a solution to counter the lack of proficient schools in certain areas of the city. The author was J. Anthony Lukas and the name of the book was *Common Ground*, which won a Pulitzer Prize for General Non-Fiction. My wife and I agreed to hold a book review discussion session at our home in Charlestown with J. Anthony Lukas and a dozen or so of our neighbors. It was a chance for them to meet Mr. Lukas and a chance for him to get some opinions, first impressions and feedback on his book from the people who lived through this controversial time in Boston's history.

Two weeks after his call, I reached out to prospective invitees around Charlestown and told them of the upcoming gathering and asked them to read *Common Ground*.

The night of the get together, twelve of my friends and neighbors gathered at my home to discuss Lukas's book with him and give him their opinions. The attendees were all residents of Charlestown. Several of them were parents with children that were directly or indirectly affected by busing. All of them were articulate and expressive in their book reviews.

In the beginning, Mr. Lukas gave an introduction and explained why he decided to write the book about busing in Boson. After he completed his commentaries about his book, he welcomed the members of the gathered group to express their opinions. The first to offer comments was a middle-aged mother of four girls, aged nineteen, eighteen, seven and six. She quickly stated that her girls were not directly affected by the busing situation because they attended parochial schools, however, she pointed out that her two younger girls had friends who attended public schools and were bused to other parts of the city. "My girls are at parochial schools, but my daughters' friends who attend public school are bused five miles away to Roxbury, which is a largely black neighborhood. Why has this happened? These girls are fearful of going so far away. Almost every other day there is a new sickness and they ask to stay home. Why do we have busing here? There is no such thing in surrounding cities. Why must we in Charlestown bear the responsibility of the insufficient Boston Public School System by exchanging our kids for those of the surrounding communities? It's not just a Boston problem; it's a challenge for all communities in Massachusetts."

It was clear that it was a regional problem, but we were paying the price for it as a city. All our neighborhood friends periodically nodded their heads in support of her points. Mr. Lukas would occasionally and politely interrupt her and others' comments with the difficulty of fully understanding the general history of Charlestown and the City of Boston, but for the most part he found their comments enlightening.

Our session ended about an hour after beginning. Mr. Lukas was patient enough to autograph copies of his book. It was a memorable evening all around! Everyone was polite and respectful to Mr. Lukas, but their general attitude was clear: "Why should we have to bear the burden of this unfair social treatment, while other communities outside of Boston were spared?" Already, many families with school-aged children were moving out of Charlestown to other communities to avoid busing. It was a tough time in Charlestown.

Before the evening ended. Anthony Lukas was asked if he was planning any other books about Boston. He said he had considered doing a book about Richard Cardinal Cushing but when he went to the archdiocesan archives he was informed there were no personal notes or letters in the archives. He was later informed that the Cardinal, before he died, had burned them.

Ted Kennedy Mends Broken Fence

In the fall of 1988, Ted Kennedy invited me to the Boston College/Army game in Dublin. The morning of the game, the local Dublin sponsoring group provided an enormous breakfast for the hundreds of American BC boosters. Later that evening, we were hosted again by Irish business leaders at a magnificent banquet. At that evening event, sitting at Ted's table was a wealthy banker from New Jersey who had just purchased a country house in Western Ireland. He bubbled about the isolation and the remoteness of his new Irish home. Ted patiently listened to his excited narration about the quietude and remoteness of his newly acquired vacation home. Finally, Ted nodded to our dinner companion and said, "I have traveled throughout much of Europe, parts of Asia and Africa, but I must admit in my recent campaign in Massachusetts, I visited Gerry's home in western Massachusetts, which I have served for many years. I thought I knew every inch of my constituency. I was amazed at the remoteness, the quietude and the country stillness surrounding his home with dense forest. I thought Daniel Boone was going to emerge from the woods." We all laughed. It was a pleasant night.

Sometime after our trip to Dublin, Ted had a series of outstanding speakers at breakfast events at the Kennedy Library. One of the most moving and unforgettable sessions was when about three hundred attendees gathered to hear from the Governor of Puerto Rico, Anibal Acevedo Vila. He was a physician who trained in Boston. He had two sisters who attended and graduated from Our Lady of the Elms College in Chicopee, which was my wife Marilyn's alma mater. An impressive number of political dignitaries were in attendance.

The event started with the most remarkable and memorable introduction. "I must digress," Ted said. "I must first thank the Governor for his appearance here today, one of Massachusetts outstanding leaders who was close to my brother the President, and who accomplished great achievements in education, labor and human rights. He was one of President Kennedy's closest friends and allies. The annals of Massachusetts legislative history are replete with his name and accomplishments. Let me present him to the gathering. He needs no introduction. The man to whom so many owe so much. My family always found him to be faithful. My good friend, Maurice Donahue." Instantly the crowd rose in unison. There was thunderous applause. Maurice rose from his table and walked up and shook Ted's hand. Shouts reverberated, "Maurice, Maurice." It was a day of reconciliation. It was the first time the two had spoken since they had a falling out several years before when Ted told Maurice he had no chance of beating Edward McCormack in the race for Governor. That morning they were together again. A great team had been united.

By this time, I was only superficially involved in politics. My major focus was my law business but I helped various candidates financially. Over the years, starting in the late sixties, I became very friendly with Joe Timilty, a young activist from Dorchester. His uncle, Joe Timilty, was very friendly with the Kennedys. After Ted's father, Joe, died, the elder Joe Timilty often escorted Ted's mother to various events and dinners. Young Joe Timilty was elected to the Boston City Council in 1967. Ted asked me to help him and I did. Eventually he ran for mayor against Kevin White, and came close to beating him.

A few years later, Timilty ran for state senator in a district that included Dorchester, Hyde Park, Sharon and Norwood. He won the seat and served from 1972 to 1985. In 1982, the state legislature had to approve an expansion of the Boston City Council, which changed the way Boston elected its city councilors. Its nine "at-large" or citywide seats became four at-large and nine district seats. Timilty's vote of approval helped to create the Hyde Park council seat for longtime aide and lifelong Hyde Park resident Tom Menino, who claimed he never could have won a citywide race. As luck would have it, Menino was Boston City Council President in 1993 when Mayor Ray Flynn left office to become Ambassador to Rome – making Menino the acting Mayor of Boston. Menino ran for the office just four months later and won. Menino, who went on to become Boston's longest serving mayor, claims he never would have won the election had he not been acting mayor.

In Menino's early years in office, John Cullinane, a very successful businessman, and I aided him. We helped Menino raise money and support in his first mayoral campaign. As Menino became busy running the city and I continued to be very active in building housing across the state, we saw less of each other. Although circumstances caused us to drift apart, I continued to support him and he always took my calls. My greatest accomplishment with Menino was pushing him to earn a degree at UMass Boston. He was a great mayor and a good friend.

Kennedy Library Foundation

For twenty-five years, in addition to my involvement in the housing development business, I co-chaired the Kennedy Library Foundation's annual May Dinner to raise money for the support of the facility. John Cullinane served as my first co-chair and was a wonderful help. Over the years, he and I, as chairmen, raised millions of dollars for the support of the Kennedy Library through these annual dinners and other fundraising events. As the years went by, Ted requested that I serve as the permanent co-chair, which I did for 25 years, and introduce a different guest co-chair each year to head the May Dinner. These honorary co-chairs included the likes of many businessmen, politicians and leaders, such as Bob Kraft and Kenneth Feinberg, among many notable others.

In 1999, a group of my friends in Charlestown worked hard to support a Catholic Charlestown grade school that was always faced with money problems. We were charged with raising money to keep our Catholic school open. As one of the directors of the Kennedy Library Foundation and permanent co-chair, I chose to have a fundraiser at the Kennedy Library to financially help the school. After cajoling and pleading with the library's designated caterer, he gave us his best price of twenty-five dollars per plate for the fundraiser. Some thought that was high but we forged ahead. It was a very simple buffet of ham and spaghetti.

We sold about three hundred tickets, but some of our committee members were not happy that the planned dinner was meager. Some told me to be ready for complaints, but we went ahead with the function. The night before our Charlestown function, a wealthy Arab Sheik sponsored a dinner at the Kennedy Library. A member of his family was being treated at Mass General Hospital. The Arab prince provided a scrumptious dinner for his friends, whom he invited from various parts of the United States, and his menu was lavishly extravagant. It was a feast for over four hundred wealthy Arabs, and included steak, chicken and all sorts of other exotic and expensive foods.

The caterer for the Arab Sheik was given an order to spare no expense. A feast of shellfish, lobster claws, and crabs was also included. Just before the Sultan's banquet, the caterer was wisely told to remove all the shellfish items from the menu, as there was an Arab dietary custom that did not permit the eating of shellfish. However, the Sheik told the caterer not to worry and that he would pay for the extra items regardless. The caterer held over all the shellfish for the next night, including it on our Charlestown menu as a gift from the Arabs. At our school function, we were delighted with the unexpected menu. Needless to say, the added treat of lobster, crabs, oysters and clams is still remembered today by many supporters of Charlestown Catholic. As one member of our committee jocularly mused, it was some sort of miracle.

In 2001, there was an opening for a director of the JFK Library Foundation. Fortunately, it was quickly filled with the recruitment of John Shattuck, who at that time was Vice President of Government, Community and Public Affairs at Harvard University. He was a graduate of Yale University and Yale Law School. He brought with him two skilled professionals from Harvard Graduate School of Education: Sandra Sadeca and Ariadne Vassalmas. As a team, they were very effective. John kept every day busy.

At first I was skeptical about how Shattuck would pan out, but as time went on I was proven wrong. He brought with him new ideas and plans for raising money. For example, before his arrival, the Foundation Group would have three outstanding speakers come to the library and address a special attendance group of five hundred people. Shattuck doubled the number of these special events and scheduled more well-known speakers to come to the library. Also, Shattuck invited about two dozen active leaders of the business community and political circles to attend these purposeful programs. After the formal program, these invitees would attend a dinner up on the sixth floor. At these gatherings, we would raise more money by enlisting these new invitees as dedicated donors. The involvement of these social dinners and notable invitees greatly enhanced the reputation of the library as a medium of stimulating public policy efforts. Over the many years of John Shattuck's oversight, the library earned the reputation as a center for inspiration and accomplishment for new policies and social achievement.

After nearly ten years of dynamic accomplishment in social and political areas, John left to become President and Rector of Central European University in Budapest, Hungary. George Soros, a businessman and philanthropist, funded an institution to develop leadership programs for the countries emerging from the control of Russia. It served as an incubator for young leaders to emerge from the Central European Countries. Through John's efforts, he created leadership to help these countries begin to take their respective positions in the free world.

My Final Thoughts

Shortly after the annual May Dinner to support the activities at the John F. Kennedy Library in 2008, Ted suffered a seizure in Hyannis and a second one on the way to Cape Cod Hospital. A couple of days later at Mass. General Hospital, doctors discovered a cancerous tumor in his brain. Now, Ted's former Chief of Staff, Doctor Lawrence C. Horowitz, came back to Hyannis and Boston to be of assistance to Ted. He organized a body of medical specialists to research procedures to pursue the best course of action.

On June 2, 2008, I was interviewed about Ted's condition by The Boston Globe. I said, "Horowitz is great, he will organize the best course of treatment for Ted. He is a double bonus because he is a medical man and a friend of Teddy." He had gathered information about all the best places for Ted to receive treatment. Late that afternoon, Horowitz and his advisors chose Duke University in North Carolina. His surgery was performed by Dr. Allan Friedman of Duke Medical Center.

After about two months of convalescence, on August 25, 2008, Ted appeared at the Democratic National Convention. Back at Hyannis, he took things very easy. However, on September twenty-sixth he suffered a mild seizure and went to the Cape Cod hospital, but could go home later that day.

While attending the Obama inauguration in January of 2009, he suffered another seizure and was taken to the Washington Hospital, but was later released to his home in Virginia. Soon after he escaped to his Florida home. On February 9, 2009, Ted returned to the Senate to vote on President Obama's stimulus package. On April 7, at the Red Sox season opener, he threw out the first pitch.

On August 25, 2009, my good friend Ted Kennedy passed away. The next day, on his website, I posted my comments: "He was a wonderful friend and a wonderful leader. He gave me a great opportunity. He was always prompted to give people a chance or to give someone a hand. No matter who you were, he was there to give you a hand. He was always concerned about the little guy. We've lost a great friend, and America has lost a great champion." On August 27, Ted lay in repose from 6:00 p.m. to 11:00 p.m. at the Kennedy Library. His wife, Vicki, gave my wife Marilyn and me the privilege of sitting with his body for the first hour.

A celebration of Ted's life took place on August twenty-ninth. The funeral service was held at Mission Church in Roxbury, known as Our Lady of Perpetual Help Basilica.

As I left the Kennedy Library after the vigil and memorial service, I had one recurring thought. There were three; now there were none. They were good men, not perfect men. Each was committed to public service as a means to make a difference. Each had an indelible impact on the history of this country. It was my privilege to have been called a friend by each of them. They changed my life.

Ted was the brother with whom I had the most contact. From his first venture into politics, I saw him transform from a somewhat entitled young man into a senator whose passion was to ensure quality healthcare was available to all, particularly those who could not afford it. That passion was borne of his own pain following a plane crash, and his son's struggle against cancer. It was borne of a realization that despite his privilege, he could empathize with others not so privileged.

I do not think Ted was ever given the credit for his hard work as a campaigner and his constant thirst for knowledge. As the years went by, Ted Kennedy loved to campaign and would talk to everyone and anyone in trying to get another vote. He was constantly learning about the latest developments in health care and other issues of the day. When meeting a constituent, he would say something like, "How are you, Charlie Brown? What a great looking tie. Can I buy it off you?" He liked people and these encounters energized him like nothing else.

I witnessed many generous and private acts of help that Ted extended to people. He always said they should remain private; he did not want any publicity. I do not think there is anyone who knew of all his acts of generosity. A memorial posted after his death recounts just one of his private acts of generosity, which I think is typical. Joan Lambert of Hyde Park, Massachusetts, wrote:

When I was a young girl and my mother struggled on Mother's Aid (welfare), she wrote to Ted and told him she had no money for our Thanksgiving or Christmas......He sent a huge box of everything, from turkey to nuts. Then at Christmas a huge box was delivered to us; it was toys, puzzles and a doll and so much more. That gave my mother so much hope where there was so much despair. Thank you for thinking of us in our time of need.

The Annual Call

Every March 17th a call would come into my office and a booming voice with a brogue would inquire, "Is Gerard there?" My receptionist would ask, "Who is calling?" The response, in the same booming voice, was always the same: "This is Ted, calling to wish Gerard a Happy St. Patrick's Day." Robin Donahue was the first receptionist to receive this call and she made sure her successors were informed about it. As the years went on, it became an expected call and it always came.

One of the best tributes I ever heard about Ted Kennedy was from an opponent, Paul Sullivan, a talk-show host who was opposed to much of what Ted Kennedy was proposing. After John Kerry lost the Presidential race, Paul Sullivan was asked by a reporter about Kerry's future in politics. He answered, "Well, he should look at Kennedy and see what Kennedy did after he lost his race for President. Ted worked at it. I don't agree with many of the things that Kennedy does, but I'm certainly convinced that at this very minute he is working for me. He is really working at it."

We did disagree about some issues, and when we did I would remind him of what Jack Kennedy once said: that he could fill Fenway Park with the people who agree with him, but he liked to talk to the people who disagreed with him.

Empathy was not enough. Ted was determined to make whatever changes in the law necessary to accomplish his goal of universal, quality healthcare for all. To do that, he had to work with others in his own party and those of the Republican persuasion. He thus became known as the *Lion of the Senate*.

I shared Ted's journey and it took me on a journey to places I could never have imagined as a young boy growing up in Charlestown.